E L

Au

KISSING
TOADS

A CHRISTIAN GIRL'S GUIDE
TO DATING AND FALLING IN LOVE

CONTENTS

SECTION TWO: INTRODUCTION

SECTION THREE: INTRODUCTION

A NOTE FROM ELIZABETH

And we know that to them that love God all things work together for good, even to them that are called according to his purpose.
Romans 8:28

Dear Friend,

As a daughter of the Amazon Rainforest, I have discovered the fairytale hidden inside of us. Each person has the opportunity to live out this fairytale as God has intended. This fairytale life is better than any story ever told. What we are searching for is not found in the things of this world, but is found in Christ. He is just waiting for us to live it out. If we are to be honest, can't we say that one of the things we look for most in life is contentment? I have learned that contentment is, in fact, the journey of the life we have with Jesus Christ.

A lot has happened between my first sloppy kiss and the intimate, God-ordained kiss shared on my wedding day. During this time, I lived and shared many crazy adventures, hard struggles, and beautiful triumphs. Consequently, all of this has molded me into the woman I am today. So, let us challenge ourselves to new heights and live the way GOD created us to live. This will bring us to a new level in Christ and will allow Jesus to mold us into what He has called us to be—in His Image.

Just like any relationship that grows into a love story, it must be cultivated. You will be required to make a sacrificial commitment and have the resilience to never quit. Never look back to the world behind you. Only by looking at the cross before you will you acquire the beautiful story God has written for your life. We must come to the foot of the cross and die to all desires of this world. As we take up our cross and crucify our flesh, let us vow to say yes to Jesus and no to sin.

My prayer is that you will become a beautiful bride for Jesus. His unconditional love will never fail you. May you discover your worth and value as you walk in purity. Our Christ is the ultimate example. Never stop spending time with your Creator. May your journey be with intent and purpose. Let your light shine so bright that the world will witness Christ in you. Go and live your life for Jesus. You won't regret it!

Join me as I have discovered my fairytale. It started when I committed my heart to Jesus, the lover of my soul. He is the King of Kings. He is dressed in dazzling clothes. His majesty is standing before you asking for your hand in marriage. God is proposing to you. Will you say yes? Will you marry Him and accept His great inheritance? Jesus Christ who saves has set aside blessings for you. All you need to do is get a hold on His blessings and enjoy the ride.

As you are reading this you may be sipping on your favorite coffee or even lying in bed. No matter where you are or what you are doing, I pray you press into these words I have shared. Thank you so much for taking the time to join hands with me as we pursue the heart of Jesus. In Christ, your adventure awaits. Let us join in unity and vow to stay pure in this 21st Century culture. This is where our true fairytale comes to life. May God bless you and your journey to become conformed to the image of Jesus Christ.

Your Friend,

Elizabeth

CHAPTER ONE

WHEN I KISSED A TOAD

B rave settlers slashed through the thickness of the Amazon Forest using only machetes and hatchets, and making way for the few natives to build and grow their crops near the Madeira River. Mud huts eventually turned into solid brick homes. After years of deforestation under the unforgiving heat and humidity, the small town of Humaitá was established in 1890. Nearly sixty years later, my missionary grandparents were the first in my family to discover this little town tucked away in the vast state of Amazonas, Brazil.

Missionary work around the world, part of my family legacy for over seventy years now, began when newlyweds Jennings and Sarah (eventually my dad's parents), decided to set sail in 1948. These two forged into the unknown jungle with little more than the clothes on their backs. Faith-filled and obedient to the call of God, they were first in the line of courageous missionaries on the Williams family tree, and because of their work, Humaita was a town where many came to a new-found life in Jesus. This city cradles my grandmother's burial site, she went to be with Jesus on October 16, 1976. I don't think she would want it any other way.

Because of my grandparent's valor to trailblaze unchartered territories, the door was open for the next generation to follow in their footsteps. My Dad, like my Grandpa, said yes to the harsh missionary life in the 1970's and was willing to carry on the much-rewarded work.

My Mom and Dad never do anything half-way (I'd like to say I inherited this trait). In a period of five years as they started their journey in the jungles, Mom gave birth to FIVE kids! Can you imagine raising all those babies in the middle of uncultivated surroundings? I don't know how she did it. As a mom of only three young kids, I struggle when my social media feed takes more than half a second to load. I know: #firstworldproblems. My parents were far from first world…I'm wondering if jungle living even makes the cut for third world?

I'm a twin, and there is exactly one year between my oldest brother and "the twins." Mom said it was as if she had triplets. We lived in the Amazon jungle for many years, and I was blessed to work alongside my parents as they taught many people about the love of Jesus. Eventually we left the primitive life and moved to Humaità. My grandparents had shared the Gospel of Jesus in this same town.

Like Tarzan when he moved to England, city life seemed a bit foreign, but as a young teen it didn't take too long for me to adjust to my new way of life. I do remember having a lot of power outages in our home, because the local officials would sell off the fuel for personal gain, leaving residents scrambling for their kerosene lamps. How frustrating it was for the settlers, but I was a teenager, and it didn't bother me too much. I was more interested in having friends and trying to fit in than worrying about going to sleep in the dark or the food spoiling in the refrigerator.

The main reason we moved to the city of flickering lights, was to start a new church plant. My parents were passionate about raising up the next generation, launching young and thriving churches wherever we settled. Soon after our start-up meetings, news spread across town about the new up and coming church (our church), which of course attracted a ton of young people. Because my parents were one of the Lead Pastors, a huge target was placed on my back as the next available Bachelorette in town. I was no longer in the obscurity of the rainforest with critters as my neighbors, but instead I was now in the spotlight. It was like living in a gigantic glass bowl, my every move (good and bad ones), became known to everyone. And so, this brings us to my very first kiss, on my very first date. All in the attempt to date me, one gutsy guy pressed through the crowds of acquaintances, into my inner circle and my family. Unfortunately, this first date did not play out as I had imagined. Sadly, my fairy tale dreams of falling in love with a prince were squelched by a toad. Without any further ado, I must share my first failed attempt at dating.

CHAPTER TWO

TRUST HIM
WITH YOUR HEART

"Above all else, guard your heart, for everything you do flows from it."
Proverbs 4:23 NIV

So, I've told you about that awful first kiss. Now, let me share with you the moments that followed: The Walk of Shame. My friends stood as eager witnesses in a courtroom waiting for a verdict. They were ready to see the new couple come out of the dark as if a kiss would seal the deal and elevate our official status to "in a relationship."

The moment I saw them, I put on a big smile pretending it was all good. But inside, I was shaking, uncomfortable inside my own skin. I just wanted to go home. The beauty of nature was no longer in sight. My senses were blocked and my thoughts were swimming in confusion. As we began to walk, their conversations sounded distant and muffled as if they were hundreds of feet away. I could only focus on my feet as I counted each step along what I felt was a highway of shame and defeat. In order to hide my disappointment, every few minutes I would smile and pretend I was enjoying the moment.

Finally, I saw the dirt driveway to my house and Dad's big white bus parked by the back door. After a quick goodbye hug, I sprinted to my room, making sure to shut the door behind me. I quickly locked it just in case a toad would try to slime its way into my bedroom. With each passing moment, the walls around my heart were going up like a brick wall. As I sat on the edge of my bed, I longed for darkness to over-shadow my feelings of loss and remorse. It wasn't just hugs and kisses, a piece of my heart was taken, and my first kiss, forever gone.

A few days later, after no response from me, my ex-boy-friend sent his buddy to my house with an important message. He was still very interested in dating me, and couldn't under-stand what went wrong. He wanted to know if there was a chance he could see me again? My look of disgust answered that loud and clear.

"But why not? What's wrong with him, Elizabeth?!" his buddy rebutted, hoping I would change my mind. He really wanted to bring good news to the TOAD.

"My answer is still no; I don't ever want to see him again."

I suddenly realized something that day. Every intimate act with a boy, no matter how small, was the same as giving away a piece of my heart. Each dream I shared, each kiss I gave, and each touch I offered was presenting a piece of ME to him. A piece I could never take back. I needed to make certain beforehand that the recipient of those precious gifts was worthy of my trust and emotions.

Just because you can give pieces of your heart away, doesn't mean you should. While waiting, it's best to keep your heart in God's hands—whole and complete. Your heart is not meant to be broken into pieces like crumbs to a beggar. I temporarily took my heart from the safety of God's hands and placed it in a boy's trust hoping to find love. My reward was the Walk of Shame with an added dose of Regret.

There is always a first for everything, but so often we take matters into our own hands to make that 'first' happen as soon as possible. Everyone around me is having their firsts… why shouldn't I? So instead of trusting God to bring that 'first' in His timing and with the right guy, I began my quest for that someone who could care for my heart, not realizing I was looking for "Prince Charming" among toads. I needed to find someone who not only loved Jesus unconditionally, but who also respected me enough that he would never steal a piece of my heart. And truth be told, before any guy ever kissed my virgin lips, God had already been intentional in the pursuit of winning my heart. As you read this next section, open up your heart, because I bet if you listen deeply, you will realize some of the same whispers have been echoing within your own heart.

TRUST YOUR HEART TO GOD

Long before I came into being, the Creator took calculated measures to make provision for my encounter with love. I didn't stumble upon unconditional love. He chose me, first. Long ago—over two thousand years ago—Jesus died on the cross for my sins, so that I could be a recipient of perfect love through the gift of Salvation. And my Savior planned to one day show up at the doorsteps of my childlike heart and ask me on a date. I said yes, and the beginning of a great romance was birthed between God and me.

I'll never forget the day I gave Him my heart and He flooded my tiny body with His love. It not only felt real, but also from that moment, I began to know God in a personal way. Since the moment I prayed and asked Him to come into my heart, I was saved, and I never doubted that I was Heaven bound. My relationship with God began to grow, and His constant presence in my life gave me a sense that I was never alone. God not only became my Savior but also the King of my heart. If I could trust Him to take care of my soul for all eternity…how much more could I trust Him to guide me through each season of my life? And this includes dating!

After my "kissing toad" experience, I knew I needed to be more careful. First, I needed to keep my heart in God's hands, knowing it was the safest place on earth. Second, before I'd say yes to dating again, I needed to go to God first and ask His opinion on the matter. God wanted to be a part of the process of when to date and who to date. He didn't want to sit this one out because He desired to walk with me through each day and every experience. And the same goes for you, too! God is waiting for you to entrust Him with your whole life and your whole heart. You can trust God with your heart, because He created you, formed you and spoke you into existence.

Have you ever tried to create something, out of nothing, using the sheer power of your words? I would love to have that kind of power, wouldn't you? I know I can't create by simply speaking, but I know my Heavenly Father can. I've read about how God created the planet out of nothing and did it all by the power of His word. He also formed the natural world in six days. The sun, the moon, all the 50 billion stars, plus the ones scientists are still counting. That's difficult for our brains to fathom, but that shouldn't keep us from believing. How marvelously breath-taking it must have been when He formed Creation, an extravagant depiction of power as He spoke the world into existence. And I haven't even gotten to the part when He made man and woman.

Imagine *that* with me for a second. I'd like to think even the angels stood in amazement at what was about to take place. God, in all Glory and Power, came to the firmament of earth and used His hands to create Adam and Eve. At the root of our being, what was formless began to take form. His word reads, "He formed man from the dust of the ground, and breathed into his nostrils the breath of life" (Genesis 2:7,22 NIV). Imagine God breathing the breath of life and using His hands to create. Just like clay in the hands of a potter, humanity was taking shape.

The psalmist wrote it so beautifully, "For You formed my inward parts; You wove me in my mother's womb. I will give thanks to You, for I am fearfully and wonderfully made; Wonderful are Your works, and my soul knows it very well" (Psalm 139:13-14, NIV). King David had a heart revelation of who created him, and how magnificent a being he was.

Once I began to wrap my mind around these truths, I came to realize that my worth was not measured by who accepted me, or which boy would choose to love me. Never again would I find myself pinned against a shed in an Amazon forest being kissed by some random guy. Not a good tradeoff from the love and acceptance I had already been given by my Heavenly Father. Happily, the same is true for you. Your worth is not in who accepts you and which boy will love you. Your heart doesn't deserve to be played with, like the game, He Loves Me, He Loves Me Not.

Who has your heart? Whoever holds your heart has your attention and focus. I believe that's why God asks us to love Him with ALL our heart. Matthew 22:37 NIV reads, "Jesus replied, "'You must love the Lord your God with all your heart, all of your soul, all of your mind.'" He wants you to choose Him first, above all others. You can trust God with your heart, because He *formed* you, because He *created* you, and because He *spoke* you into existence.

Maybe at this point, you have already given away hugs and kisses as I did. And perhaps in your failed attempt to receive love and acceptance, you caved. Statistically, you're that teen who has gone past your personal boundaries of respect and self-worth, giving away your body and purity prematurely—outside the boundaries of marriage. If this is you, I want to encourage you. It's not too late. There is no decision you have made in the past that can disqualify you for God's best for your future.

First, know your enemy. As we have read in Ephesians, it clearly depicts the villain. "For our struggle is not against flesh and blood, but against the rulers, against the powers, against the world forces of this darkness, against the spiritual forces of wickedness in the heavenly places" (Ephesians 6:12, NASB).

The enemy wants you to believe there is no way you can make things right again. That once you've given away your body by sinning, God wants nothing to do with you. And then the devil continues, whispering constant lies, telling you that God doesn't want your heart and body restored. He deceives you as he convinces you that it's too late, you are damaged goods. If you are in this trap and are feeling like you're worthless, look up, because there is hope! Look up to your Heavenly Father, for He sees you and He loves you *unconditionally!*

Your Heavenly Father is on your side, and He wants to take you out of hopelessness. There is nothing your God can't heal, mend, and make brand-new. Let's not forget how He miraculously formed you. If He formed you into existence, He can restore you into right standing. Give God your hurting heart, body and soul, because He's trustworthy. Let God do what only He can do as your Savior and Father. You can trust Him with your heart again. Recommit your life to Jesus, or commit to Him for the first time. It's never too late to get back up, dust yourself off, and put your heart where it belongs: in the hands of Jesus. This is the safest place on earth.

Whether you've never given away a kiss, gone past a kiss or two, or way beyond, there is one thing we have in common. We have a Heavenly Father who cares about us, who took the time to form us into existence. We can trust Him with our hearts. And, as far as kissing toads is concerned, we most certainly can trust in Him to orchestrate the perfect timing for kissing and dating. And when we do, we can be absolutely certain that when He says the time is "right" the gentleman on the other end will be "right" as well!

Place your heart in His hands and wait for His perfect timing.

QUESTIONS FOR YOU TO CONSIDER

———

1. Have you ever been kissed for the first time or been on a first date? If so what was it like for you?
2. Has your heart been broken?
3. Have you given your heart to Jesus? If so, describe your experience.

MY CONFESSION

———

God, I give you my whole heart before I give it away to anyone else. Because I am special in your sight help me to guard my heart and be choosy about who has access to it. I am magnificent and holy through Christ Jesus. My purpose is greater than me, and because of it, I am set apart. Because I have an intimate and personal relationship with God, I am already affirmed, accepted and approved.

MY PRAYER

———

Heavenly Father, I recognize that my identity is found in Christ Jesus. I give my heart to you as my first true love. I want you as my Lord and Savior, and to be the one who holds my heart as I save it for that someone special. Give me courage and strength to say no when I need to stand up and do what is right for me.

CHAPTER THREE

CHOOSE TO WAIT

Even though I was only fifteen years old, meeting "the one" was already in my field of dreams. When I said yes to my insistent friends to go on my first date, I was secretly hoping to meet my future husband. Clearly, he wasn't quite the prince I had envisioned. I was rudely awakened to the reality I had kissed a toad. Kissing the wrong guy made an impression on my life as a single girl. This was not how I had imagined my first kiss to be, much less, how I had dreamed of one day meeting my future husband.

After my bad date went south, I gave myself a time out from dating, and I chose to wait. I had failed at doing it my way and my friends' way, and I needed a new strategy plan. So I figured the best way for me to stay safe, and free from headaches would be to close the door to my heart, put a lock on it, and hide the key. I chose to let love lie dormant until I could handle it.

Girls, I realize this is totally counter-culture. Especially for your generation! At the youngest ages, all of you have been watching Disney movies and shows where very young girls are kissing boys. In all your tweet and teen magazines, the covers are littered with promises about how to attract and keep the right boy. There is no respect given to waiting…that seems absurd! In a culture where we can microwave dinners in 3 minutes, find any information we need online in .03 seconds, and instantly text our communications 24/7, waiting for anything is a colossal waste of time! But, let me reassure you, no matter what your culture is screaming at you, the truth is this: Timing is everything.

Timing is what we all seem to struggle with when it comes to relationships. "Why can't I just find the right guy?" "Am I ever going to have my first kiss?" And then once we find a guy, "If this relationship were just a few more years from now, it would be perfect," we complain to our girl-friends. Timing seems to be that third party who's always there disrupting your ideal plans.

Here is a good general rule of thumb: The guy you meet at the wrong time, most likely, is not the one for you. God has set seasons in place because there is an appointed time for everything, including when to pursue love. Ecclesiastes 3 (NASB) says it best:

There is an appointed time for everything. And there is a time for every event under heaven—

A time to give birth and a time to die;
A time to plant and a time to uproot what is planted.
A time to kill and a time to heal;
A time to tear down and a time to build up.
A time to weep and a time to laugh;
A time to mourn and a time to dance.
A time to throw stones and a time to gather stones;
A time to embrace and a time to shun embracing.
A time to search and a time to give up as lost;
A time to keep and a time to throw away.
A time to tear apart and a time to sew together;
A time to be silent and a time to speak.
A time to love and a time to hate;
A time for war and a time for peace.

After reading the sequence of time, one can easily conclude that God is a God of order. He will never send you things at the wrong time to trip you up. If the timing is wrong, then there's a good chance the guy isn't your soulmate. Let's take it a step further. If he isn't the one, then why even entertain it? What if he is someone else's future husband?

You may be thinking right about now, "Slow down, I am not looking for a serious relationship." You even call it, "just friends," so mom and dad won't panic. But, whatever base you're on: first, second or third, it all counts. At any point, you are exchanging your feelings, entertaining thoughts in your mind of you falling in love with him and that's a big deal. Once you begin to entertain dating, you must become aware that you have nominated yourself to walk down a slippery slope.

Once you're faced with the pressures of dating (unsupervised), you can end up awakening love prematurely. At such a young age, it's very hard to have self-control, if not impossible. As a young couple spending lots of time together, falling in love is inevitable. The pull towards each other emotionally and physically is hardly without restraint. If you play with fire, you risk getting burnt. If you play with love and romance, casual dating at the wrong time, with the wrong person, you risk doing things you'll regret later.

When I chose to wait, it didn't mean I was suddenly numbed to love. Here's a news flash for you, girls: God created love, not pop culture. God made you and me "to love and be loved," and there is absolutely nothing bad about it. Let's not throw away what is good and perfect, the longing to be loved, as though it's a bad thing for Christian girls to desire. After all, I was still a teen girl dreaming to one day meet my Prince Charming. But, I needed to come to grips with myself and trust God's timing. It IS possible to be single and NOT desperate. At the right time, I knew the right one would show up, because falling in love was always a part of God's will for my life.

Wait. Trust me, you will never regret it.

Wait to date even if the desire is strong and the pressure is unbearable. I promise it will be worth it. Dating should not be taken lightly because when boy meets girl and sparks begin to fly, this always leads to something. Save "dating" for when you're ready to pursue marriage.

You see, marriage has a bigger purpose than two people expressing their love for one another. Marriage also serves as an example of how God pursues us. God stands as the groom before humanity, asking her to marry Him. The picture of Jesus hanging on the cross with arms open wide declaring to us all, "if you marry me, if you accept me as your Savior, everything that I have is yours, and I will love you forever."

Romans 8 is a great depiction of God's unconditional love for His bride: "He who did not spare His own Son, but delivered Him over for us all, how will He not also with Him freely give us all things? Who will bring a charge against God's elect? God is the one who justifies; who is the one who condemns? Christ Jesus is He who died, yes, rather who was raised, who is at the right hand of God, who also intercedes for us. Who will separate us from the love of Christ? Will tribulation, or distress, or persecution, or famine, or nakedness, or peril, or sword?" (Romans 8:31-39, NASB)

It takes maturity from both a man and a woman to build a marriage that is worthy to be a reflection and an example of how God loves His bride. I know looking back, I was not ready to get married at fifteen, meaning I was not ready to engage in a dating relationship of any kind: casual, just friends, or however you like to phrase it. When God created you, He wired you to one day to be in a relationship by entering a covenant relationship with the man of your dreams. As you dream of one day meeting him, choose to wait. The following chapters will show you how.

While choosing to wait, become that girl who knows her season and embraces God's timing. I believe you are that girl! Meanwhile, give your love story to God. In the waiting, imagine what can happen if you use your life, the season you're in, to live intentionally and on purpose for God.

If you have gone down the slippery slope and experienced heartache, please give yourself a time-out on dating. Don't jump to the next relationship in fear your friends will label you a loser in the "dating game." It is never too late to get in sync with the rhythm of God's perfect timing. He is notorious for resetting time and giving you a fresh start.

"I chose to wait" was my strategy plan, and it worked. Waiting to date ended up being the best option for me, I avoided a lot of unnecessary headaches that comes with dating. I chose to close the door to my heart—not awaken love until it so desired—which is talked about in Song of Solomon 8:4.

If you know that God is for you, and wants to protect you from unnecessary pain then wait and trust God's divine calendar. Recognize the season of singleness (going solo, not hitched) and don't get ahead of yourself. His plan for you will come together. If falling in love is part of God's story for you remember this: At the right time, the right one will show up. God's timing is perfect. Choose to wait.

QUESTIONS FOR YOU TO CONSIDER

———

1. What are you looking for in a prince?
2. What experiences have you had this far with boys?
   If none what are you doing to prepare?
3. Why should you choose to wait?

MY CONFESSION

———

God, thank you for making me wonderful. I am made to love and be loved. I am a Christ follower who wants my life to reflect what you did on the cross. I choose you first as my love the one who completes. Because you are in me I declare that I am strong and confident as a single woman. For I am already complete in Jesus.

MY PRAYER

———

Heavenly Father, thank you for creating me so that I can be loved by you first before anyone else. Give me a healthy perspective on dating and finding the one. Help me to trust your timing and if the time isn't right give me the courage to say no. Forgive me for the times I have stepped out on my own, my life is no longer mine to lead. I make you Lord and Savior of my life.

CHAPTER FOUR

DOWN TO THE ROOTS
OF DATING

I might as well share my little secrets with you as we trek along together in this book. Here's one that has haunted me for a loooooooong time: There is a gene that runs in my family that NOBODY wants. In fact the only gene in my family tree that trumps it is the Grandma-full-moustache gene. That one is wicked because it magically pops up overnight the moment your first grandchild is born and dooms you to shave for the rest of your days, unless you plan to forego getting kisses from your grand babies. But I digress. The one I want to talk about is a close second to the girl-stache gene, and that is the white hair gene. And guess what? I inherited it from BOTH my parents. Double whammy.

I don't have a few, but LOTS of gray hairs all over my head. Seriously, if I were to pluck them all in one sitting, I'd be bald. This curse of graying prematurely has left my siblings and me to the unforeseen fate of completely white hair in our 20's. I would love to say it's all due to wisdom, but let's be honest, It's not, yawl! (in Cajun dialect) Now I'm in my thirties and I have a head full of white hair, which leaves me two options: One, join my brothers who don't seem to mind going all-natural (not a look I'm willing to take on). Or two, spend a TON of time sitting in a salon getting my roots done. Obviously, I opt for Door #2.

I used to be able to wait and go to the salon every four weeks, but not anymore. Every three weeks is a MUST for the rest of my life. My hair stylist is super talented and uses only the best and strongest coloring product on the market (which I would pay an exorbitant amount of money if you dared me to find a cure). But to no avail, I lose the battle every month of White Hair vs. Chemical. Without fail, my white hair conquers as these snow-capped roots rise again like a brigade ready for battle for all the world to see. Because there is no cure, I am forced to treat the symptom of white hair. Every. Three. Weeks. (**sigh**)

As I look at young people in the world today, I wonder if we are all approaching dating as I do my gray hair—covering up the roots and accepting the problem. Could it be we have allowed certain habits and patterns in our dating because "it's just the way it is," but never stopped to think about *why* we date the way we date? Maybe you don't even think there *is* a problem, like my frizzy roots covered in a dark brown color. But just because I can't see the grays it doesn't mean they're not there.

So, to better understand the why we date the way we date in today's world, we need to take a quick trip back in time to a period in our history when there was a cultural shift from courtship to dating. We will then fast-forward to the present day, and how casual dating has gotten so twisted. Choosing to date the way culture has accepted it since the turn of the century does come with its downfalls.

After looking at the history of dating and its downfalls, you must conclude there has to be a better way. I believe courtship is the best method of how to date for success even though it's so against the social norm. I say we take the challenge, and head on over to dissect "the roots of dating," like a scientist at a Paul Mitchell's color innovation lab. Except in this case, it's not the color or roots we are dealing with because there are somethings much more valuable at stake: our hearts.

WHEN DATING WAS FIRST INTRODUCED

———

It wasn't until the late 1800s and early 1900s that dating was introduced into our western society. Before this, a young man would respectfully ask the father of his intended if he could spend time with her, knowing these times would be completely supervised and under the watchful eyes of parents or chaperones. This type of courtship was a family affair, and everyone knew what was at stake. Every step was communicated and promises were not exchanged until there was a certainty about an upcoming nuptial.

Then young people decided they wanted a change of pace. A way to engage with the opposite sex on their own terms and without observation. Young love birds got brave, leaving mom and dad's swing on the porch, forgetting that good ole homemade sweet tea, and started to date in the public forums. Suddenly theatres, restaurants, and later, movies and diners were the playing fields of Cupid's arrows. I wonder if that's around the time root-beer floats became popular?

The concept of dating spread like wild fire consuming the hearts of passionate young people. Dating was now the new norm, the casual aspect of courtship was now acceptable. The biggest change that occurred was the number of partners a person would have before settling down and getting married. Before the wedding day, girls would have dated quite a few young men without the prospect of getting married. Dating casually, also became a new norm for pre-teens as young as twelve-year-olds partnering and dating like older couples. If you were "going steady" with someone, you fit in just fine.

Beth Bailey's book, *From Front Porch to Back Seat: Courtship in Twentieth-Century America*, says that, "By the early 1950s, going steady had acquired an entirely different meaning. It was no longer the way a marriageable couple signaled their deepening intentions. Instead, going steady was something twelve-year-olds could do, and something most fifteen-year-olds did. Few steady couples expected to marry each other (especially the twelve-year-olds), but, for the duration, they acted as if they were married. Going steady had become a sort of play-marriage, a mimicry of the actual marriage of their slightly older peers (p. 49)."2

Bailey goes on to state, "It's now a cultural norm 'to casually date' or even put into practice the modern term 'friends with benefits." Does this all sound familiar to you? Look around and you will see that casual dating is in every part of our world: movies, music, friends, the popular votes say, "Do it this way."

Dating has gotten confusing and convoluted in modern relationships, but our history points to a long unhealthy pattern that was birthed and never broken. Casual dating turned into competition; the more you competed the more popular you got...but to compete you had to date to stay on top. Bailey also says, "There was not an end: popularity was a deceptive goal. It was only a transient state, not a trophy that could be won and possessed. You competed to become popular and being popular allowed you to continue to compete. The competition was the key term in the formula–remove it, and there was no rating, dating, or popularity (pp.30-31)."3

Girls, you don't have to join this overrated society with its unhealthy habits, and risk your heart being broken for the sake of acceptance. Your life, your heart, is not for the many others. It should only be given away to that special someone God has just for you, not for your multiple guy friends. Casual dating has been acceptable as a rite of passage for many teens. However, dating among teens, as the popular activity of choice, does have its downfalls once you enter the arena of casual dating.

DOWNFALLS OF DATING

———

Let's fast forward to where we are today and address a few of the many downfalls teens face choosing to play this dating game. It's sad to know what girls and boys are yielding to. Perhaps the examples below are not a part of your personal journey, but you may know someone who is in the middle of a dating cycle who may need your help.

– 1ST DOWNFALL –
Dating without the intent of marriage.

Here's how this plays out: You are attracted to a boy and find out he is interested in you. You start getting to know each other on a friendship level, but you don't bring up the romance and long-term commitment because you are way too young. Time goes by and you start sharing way more than conversation and begin acting like a married couple. Mimicking marriage will only lead to doing marriage. If you are talking like husband and wife, sharing your feelings for each other, spending a lot of time alone, as married couples do, it is a no brainer what could happen next. Eventually, you are pushing extreme limits in the physical realm.

You then convince yourself to go along with this "lowkey casual thing" you're doing because nothing major is going to happen. You believe you have it under control. Wrong. After a few months or more of dating without the intent of marriage, the inevitable happens: one of you begins to pull away. Because long-term was never the goal, your feelings of love and attraction are leaving as fast as it entered your heart: guilt, lack of sleep, worry and fear begin to creep in. Something doesn't feel right and you know it. Your desire to get out of the relationship intensifies leaving you no choice but to end it.

Your dating experience is now expired, and it's time to move on. One is relieved, and the other is left devastated wallowing in a pool of tears. Both have given serious parts of themselves to the other, which can never be undone. Friendships can get severed, and can even put a rift between the parents or the circle of friends, because dating affects more than just the love birds. At the end of the day, there is only pain and regret.

— 2ND DOWNFALL —
Hard to stop playing the game.

You are too young to marry and at some point dating without the intent of marriage only means you will have to break it off. It hurts too much, so you promise yourself that you are not going to put yourself through that again until you know it's "right." But this is like promising yourself you will only eat ONE Oreo cookie. Come on…who can do THAT? Once that box is open and you taste the crunchy, chocolatey goodness coupled with the soft sweet icing, you know you can't enjoy just one. It's TOOOO GOOOOOOOD.

Dating is the same way. Now that you're in the dating game, having awakened your sexuality and attraction, having felt what it feels like to hug and kiss, it's difficult to stop playing. Being solo just doesn't cut it any more. The solution to stay on top of your game is to jump into another relationship. But we all know this is not a good idea. Maybe the biggest problem with the dating game is that with each passing relationship, the break-ups create more emotional scarring than the one before. You find yourself being a victim to more hurt as you pass through the emotional aftermath of yet another disappointment.

— 3RD DOWNFALL —
The lies of instant gratification.

We all suffer from the disease of now. Culture encourages us all to live our lives for the now, with no strings attached to the future. Think about how it is engrained in the fabric of our society, "If you want it, you can have it now." You can shop online and turn on the *1-click* feature and they guarantee you next day delivery. Nowadays it is instant gratification with almost everything! And the promises (or more accurately, LIES) that we believe is that once we have that thing we will be satisfied. But that is never the case. It's just like the Oreo cookie…the lingering taste only compels us to want more. Getting a boyfriend might temporarily make you feel good, but long-term this will only bring break-ups and heart-aches. Just like my white roots, while I love what my hair looks like as I walk out of the salon, it's only a matter of time before the white hairs start to pop out again. If insecurity is what is pressing you for instant gratification, even though you might get what you want it's only a matter of time before that same insecurity pops out again demanding to be covered up with a new antidote. The same goes for loneliness, a need for popularity, a need to be chosen…or whatever your motive to rush into a dating relationship.

Guard against instant gratification. Don't give your heart away like it's for sale on Amazon Prime. John Ortberg said it well: "Biblically, waiting is not just something we have to do until we get what we want. Waiting is part of the process of becoming what God wants us to be."

Trust God in the waiting. You are worth waiting for as you trust God with your heart. He is maturing you and your future spouse for when the time is right. Think about your legacy, what stories will your grand kid want hear about you? God is more interested in the process than the destination.

Casual dating doesn't have to be your initiation into society as a young woman coming of age. Casual dating wasn't for me and deep down in my heart I knew it. After my bad experience with kissing my toad, I felt there was a better and safer path. Stop to weigh the cost. Is it worth going through heartache from one bad breakup to the next? Yes, it will happen. Dating comes to a halt, you or him/or both, on the receiving end will get hurt. Do you want to be that person who ends up five years down the road having had numerous boyfriends? Just for bragging rights to talk about it with your girl-friends, but at what cost? Kiss dating goodbye.

Now that we have looked at dating and its possible downfalls over a period of one hundred years to present, we should conclude there is a better way. Read on...the next chapter will give you everything you need to know about dating in a way that will protect your heart.

QUESTIONS FOR YOU TO CONSIDER

———

1. What are your thoughts on casual dating?
2. How has casual dating affected your life or your friends?

MY CONFESSION

———

I am a girl worthy of God's best. I find the truth of who I am in God's word, the Bible, not in magazines or the opinion of others. I don't have to conform to the ways and the patterns of this world any longer. May I be the one to break the cycle of bad patterns in my family and my friends. May I influence change and not be influenced by the world. I can do this because of Christ living in me.

MY PRAYER

———

Jesus, help me to renew my mind daily and cleanse me as I pray and read the Bible. I ask as I seek you with all my heart, I will know your will is good and acceptable for me. I activate God's word over my life. I confess Romans 12:2 NASB and decree this as my prayer: "And do not be conformed to this world, but be transformed by the renewing of your mind, so that you may prove what the will of God is, that which is good and acceptable and perfect".

CHAPTER FIVE

COURTSHIP 101

May he kiss me with the kisses of his mouth!
For your love is better than wine.
Song of Solomon 1:2 NASB

I love browsing in magazines. It's kind of a guilty pleasure. What's not to like? You can see all the latest fashions, learn the newest make-up tips, and be privy to all the latest juicy news. Not that you can believe everything printed, but it's still fun to read. And it's a feast for your eyes. But I gotta tell ya, at the end of my magazine splurge, while my soul is filled with yearning for the newest pair of boots or the latest trend I MUST have, I have not gained any true wisdom for my life. Well, unless you count as wisdom how to use make up to make my eyebrows look like they have been micro-bladed.

Probably not.

The only place to gain perfect wisdom that has outlasted countless dynasties and empires over the last six thousand years is the Bible. We believe it is God's inspired Word, and within its pages are practical truths that can apply to every person, in any demographic, in any social situation, and any generation. But sometimes you have to want it because scripture doesn't always spell out your particular situation. You have to study and read between the lines. Look for patterns. Discover God's character and learn to replicate it in your life.

But unlike the bright magazines calling to you from the stands, you won't see the Bible crawling up to your lap and begging you to read its pages. It doesn't boast or brag, but if you choose to open up the Word of God it will never disappoint. While I love my fashion magazines, the information in them is not what my heart *needs*. This precious part of me requires a daily dose of wisdom and truth, and I would trust the Bible over any magazine or the voice of any top young celebrity. If you think about it the Bible has been around way longer than any Teen Cosmo or Seventeen Magazine. So I'm sure we can all agree that we should not let the magazines, social media and popular opinions be our "go to" for wisdom about when and how to date.

In the Bible, the "institution of modern-day dating" is not mentioned, this can only mean one thing: there is something else, something better. God is not silent on this subject. He made sure to cover every topic referring to all human desires, needs or wants. Whatever the answer you long for, with much study and a heart of humility, you *will* find what you are looking for in the Holy Scriptures. That's why it's critical to use the Bible as your go to life-line above all other knowledge and worldly wisdom.

Throughout the Old and New Testament, the "how to do it right" when entering a romantic relationship is treated with much regard and respect. On my quest to discover what God had to say about courtship, I ran into an incredible verse-by-verse teaching of the Song of Solomon, by Tommy Nelson. It was enlightening, to say the least. Never in a million years, would I have imagined that the Song of Solomon had so much to offer in the realm of dating, with wisdom from centuries ago about how to date God's way.

Currently I work as a volunteer, and go into schools and youth events, teaching students the importance of waiting and learning how to choose wisely. Think about it: choosing your partner for life is the second most important decision you will ever make, after Salvation. If that's the case then why not spend time educating yourself on how to choose wisely.

Sometimes I chuckle because parents can get a bit uncomfortable when I mention this little book in the Bible. When I send a note home asking moms and dads for permission to teach their High School age sons and daughters about the Song of Solomon, I have had some very interesting push-back. You see, this book is a pretty graphic love story and one that expresses the passion of courtship and marriage. But I love it because God chose to keep it in the Holy Scriptures to express to us that He is not embarrassed or shy about the passion love evokes. He wants us to be knowledgeable about this subject so we can act wisely when falling in love.

Unfortunately, by the time some parents wake up to the importance of talking to their kids on how to wait, and how to choose a soulmate, it's usually too late. I get desperate phone calls and messages all the time, moms devastated their young tween girls got exposed to things they shouldn't. I'm talking about 5th graders. Tender kids crossing boundaries outside of marriage. Devastating news for a parent to absorb. This is why I'm so passionate about being honest on these issues without turning red in the face. We must start talking about THE SECOND MOST IMPORTANT DECISION ONE WILL EVER MAKE—MARRIAGE. These topics do not have to be taboo as it was for our parents and grandparents.

And having conversation about marriage doesn't start when you are six months away from your wedding; it begins the day you start daydreaming, and falling in love in your heart before anyone knows. You may need to take the initiative and turn to Scriptures and open the dialogue with your parents or someone you trust who can give you wise counsel. Don't go through this alone! If you have no one to talk to, then please send me an email and I will do whatever I can to get you some help.

PROGRESSION

———

Going through the study by Tommy Nelson of Song of Solomon helped shape how I approached dating in the realm of courtship. There is a God-instituted progression that occurs between a man and a woman as they are nearing marriage. The Bible isn't specific to what age a person is eligible to court, but it is specific on the steps taken in the progression towards a couple's wedding ceremony. There are five steps that occur from the moment you are attracted to someone to the point that you are walking down the aisle secure in the decision you both made. Before I cover the progression, extracted from scriptures that depict the epic love story of Solomon and the Shulamite Woman, let's first define courtship in its simplest form.

What does courting really mean? Is it mentioned in the dictionary? It is a valid word and a concept worth considering. In short, courtship simply means: "A period, a set amount of time (between a man and woman) in which a couple is getting to know each other, as they're seeking to solidify God's will towards marriage." Also, courtship is a choice to wait and not give away your heart piece by piece to many others as in the dating institution: going from one relationship to the next without the intent of marriage. In contrast to dating, courtship is undertaken only when both parties are prepared, mature, and ready to pursue marriage.

If, during courtship, one or both parties realize that marrying him/her is not God's will you have no choice but to end the courtship. However, this does not mean you have failed. In fact, you have succeeded, since both were committed to seeking God's will from the beginning. And ultimately, you both have received the answer you were looking for. Courtship is also a heart attitude choosing to please God first. It's choosing to seek His perfect will when engaged in a relationship and prayerfully desiring to hear from Him whether this person is the one for you or not. Courtship is choosing to seek what the Bible says on the matter rather than the opinion of others.

— 1. ATTRACTION —

This first step is probably stating the obvious! Please, girls…it's a GOOD thing to be attracted to a boy. If there is no zing in your heart and you are just trying this out because he seems to be the perfect resume boyfriend maybe you need to take a step back.

Attraction is that undeniable, innate feeling that draws you to someone special who stands out in the crowd above all others. There is nothing new under the sun, trust me. We can trace things all the way back to the Bible. And right in the middle of the Word, we see the art of attraction jumping off the pages in the "Song of Solomon," and this couple's attraction for each other may surprise you. This little book of eight short chapters is a snapshot of a couple falling in love, which means there are two main characters in this love book, "him" and "her."

This is her response to how she felt about him: "May he kiss me with the kisses of his mouth! For your love is better than wine. Your oils have a pleasing fragrance, Your name is like purified oil; Therefore the maidens love you. (Song of Solomon 1:2-3, NASB).

This girl's got it bad. She is lying there *daydreaming* about this guy, VERY ATTRACTED to him. He is handsome and she likes the way he smells. In their culture when a woman made the comment, "your oils have a pleasing fragrance" it meant she was attracted to him. She liked his smell (no showers like today, no Dove soap for them); the people didn't often bathe, so his cologne mattered. Interesting though how she doesn't stop at skin deep. She goes on to say, "Your name is like purified oil; Therefore the maidens love you (vs.3)." This guy was very good looking, but most importantly, he had CHARACTER. His name was known and he had a good reputation in town. He was a man of valour.

And why was he attracted to her? (read on) "I am black but lovely, O daughters of Jerusalem, like the tents of Kedar, Like the curtains of Solomon. "Do not stare at me because I am swarthy, for the sun has burned me. My mother's sons were angry with me; They made me caretaker of the vineyards, But I have not taken care of my own vineyard" (Song of Solomon 1:5-6, NASB).

Girls, it says here that she was hardworking (caretaker of the vineyards). She was submissive to authority (her brothers).

Maybe her dad wasn't present and the brothers were the ones in charge. This girl had a servant's heart. She had the attractive qualities we find in a person: hardworking, submitted to authority, a servant's heart, putting others above herself.

Physical attraction is in full bloom when he says to his love, "How beautiful you are, my darling, how beautiful you are! Your eyes are like doves. How handsome you are, my beloved, And so pleasant! Indeed, our couch is luxuriant!" (Song of Solomon 1:15-16, NASB).

Just curious, what type of looks are you attracted to? What are some non-negotiable features he must have? Tall, blonde, brown eyes, blue eyes, athletic, nerdy, artsy, trendy. Who you hang with does influence how you formulate that "look" you are attracted to in a guy. Attraction is a great first step, but you can't stop there because it's not dependable. It's important to be attracted to each other, but it's not everything.

Take note of this very important statement: This step is 100% superficial! Being attracted to someone is not enough to assume he is marriage material. You don't want to be pursuing a **handsome** guy who is the biggest jerk and most irresponsible loser on campus, do you? It's obvious he is not marriage material. In short, looks aren't everything. And Proverbs 31 confirms this to be true, "Favor is deceitful, and beauty is vain: but a woman that fears the LORD, she shall be praised" (Proverbs 31:30 NASB).

— 2. THE ACCEPTANCE —

Now that we know beauty can be vain, we must cautiously take the next step. This step is when you accept the invitation to go on a date. Don't confuse an introductory date with courtship thinking it's the same as dating without the intent of marriage. When you go on a date within the concept of courtship, two people agree to meet for observation purposes only. There is no physical touch and no commitment, just the motive to get to know if that someone special is a possible prospect. You notice in the chronology of the couple's progression in Song of Solomon, there is no evidence of physical touch at this point. They are dating in the open, in public spaces. This step is filled with conversation and talking about likes/dislikes, goals, dreams, and most importantly about each of your relationships with Christ.

"My beloved is like a gazelle or a young stag. Behold, he is standing behind our wall, He is looking through the windows, he is peering through the lattice." (Song of Solomon 2:9, NASB). He compares her to a gazelle or a young stag. These animals required handling with much care and tenderness. Solomon is kind and gentle with her. He treated her with the utmost respect.

Hopefully, as you read this couple's progression it will give you an excellent example of how to choose to date. After going on a few dates, along with seeking God in prayer and talking to mature mentors, you should know if he is someone you want to pursue. Again, please remember this is not a dating game where you are constantly wondering if he is going to kiss you or hold your hand. This time with that person is with a very specific goal in mind: Is he courtship potential (marriage material), or not? May I recommend you do this openly and never behind anyone's back. If a relationship starts in secret, isolated on some blue lagoon island, hidden from parents and those who care about you, there's something not right and most likely, he's not the one.

Invite your prospect to spend time with your friends and family. I personally always planned these observation dates in group settings. Hanging out in a group environment was much more comfortable than being alone in the back of some obscure restaurant. Group functions are less pressure in case you need a way out or you realize he's not courtship material. I'd still advise you to pray before going on a first date. I might add, DO NOT get in the habit of going on dates just because you are attracted to him or flattered you were asked to go on a date. If you are doing this you may simply be playing the dating game.

– 3. THE COURTSHIP –

Once you have both prayed and have sought godly advice and you still want to proceed....Congratulations! It's official, "you are courting." However, the clock is now ticking because you have set things in motion. The courtship phase is not meant to be a long extended period of dating. You should aim for only a few months of courting if at all possible—not years of dating. There are some isolated scenarios: being in a long distant relationship, or a school or job situation which can extend the length of your courtship. But in most cases, as a rule of thumb this should be a short season. If you follow this progression from the first date to wedding day, on average, this should be a period of about six months to one year. Be honest with each other, and keep your eyes wide open…it's extremely difficult to control your passions when you are both in love and physically attracted to each other. Playing with passion is like getting dunked in gasoline and holding a box of matches, eventually you will strike one and catch on fire.

If you are thinking to yourself, *there is no way I could be married within the next six months to a year,* then it's a sure sign you should not be entertaining courtship, much less dating. You are not ready to date. If this is you, use this chapter as an opportunity to learn and prepare for when you're ready to engage in courtship. Again, I realize this concept of courtship goes against the grain of what pop culture says is okay. But before you throw this idea of courtship out the window, thinking it is way too weird, take a second to think about all the other things pop culture is saying is acceptable and cool. If you are a Christian and you have a desire to please God, I know there are many cultural trends that cause conflict in your heart. Consider that this idea of dating is no different than the other issues that go against Bible truths.

— 4. THE ENGAGEMENT —

The next step of courtship, which occurs right before marriage is the engagement phase. In our day and age, I've seen some crazy proposals. Off the top! Guys are going all out, proposing in front of thousands at football games or even on national television. In the last portion of this book I share how I was proposed to and it was quite special, so stay tuned. But please keep this in mind, engagement is more than getting an extravagant proposal and a pretty ring to wear on your finger. Engagement is all about preparing for marriage as both of you are learning the art of marriage through pre-marital counseling. Never allow yourself to skip this special counseling that will give tips on how to bring both you and your fiance together. Two lives becoming one is never easy. Always miraculous and totally worth it…but never easy.

Let's go back to the Song of Solomon. "My beloved responded and said to me, 'Arise, my darling, my beautiful one, and come along. 'For behold, the winter is past, the rain is over and gone. 'The flowers have already appeared in the land; The time has arrived for pruning the vines, and the voice of the turtledove has been heard in our land. 'The fig tree has ripened its figs, and the vines in blossom have given forth their fragrance. Arise, my darling, my beautiful one, and come along!'" (Song of Solomon 2:10-13, NASB). Her vineyard has come alive. She is flourishing. The blessing of God is evident in this relationship. But the couple CANNOT let their guards down just because they are engaged and close to marriage.

Just two verses down from the engagement is a sharp re-
minder to stand on guard against the things that can spoil the
vineyard: "Catch the foxes for us, the little foxes that are ruin-
ing the vineyards, while our vineyards are in blossom." (Song
of Solomon 2:15, NASB). The vineyard is being compared
to the relationship between the engaged couple. As stated
above, in a vineyard before there were juicy sweet grapes, the
flowers came to life and blossomed, what a sight it must have
been. Once the flowers fell off, the grapes started to form.
Caring and protecting the precious vineyard was a must. If,
however, foxes wiggled their way into the vineyard during this
tender season, they would eat the grapes prematurely and dev-
astate the entire crop. Hence, the grapes never came into full
maturity: No flowers, no grapes, no grapes, no wine.

As one who cares for the vineyard, both the girl and
the guy must guard against the little foxes that can ruin and
awaken love in the relationship before it is time—prematurely.

What can ruin a relationship? Many things can raise
an ugly head (bad habits, one not being a born-again believ-
er, etc.). But, most detrimental is premarital sex or any form
of sexual immorality. This is the most significant threat to
a relationship. Notice the pronoun "us" in the verse mentioned above; both are committed to making it work, both are
committed to purity. There is a determination to protect their
relationship. I must emphasize, if during any point in your
courtship, whether you're on your first step or engaged, if you
become doubtful, hesitant, or fearful about your decision, you
have every right to end it. Don't be afraid to break off an en-

gagement! I'm speaking from experience, as this was one of the hardest decisions I ever had to make. However, it saved me from making an even bigger mistake.

— 5. THE WEDDING —

Once you have both heard from God, if there is peace in the decision, and your loved ones and mentors are supportive, then proceed with the wedding preparations. When you try to do it right, when you desire to please God it's amazing how blessings will shower down like an unexpected summer rain. You'll be overwhelmed at the goodness of God. Have a BLAST planning your wedding. Say YES to the dress and pick your wedding party. Enjoy planning the details of the ceremony and reception. It will be a day you will never forget!

Can you see it now? When you approach courtship with the intent of marriage there is a better way and it's backed up by scriptures. The progression is easy and without turmoil, just the way God intended it to be. You deserve to have a beautiful courtship story. Don't settle for anything less. I tried dating for the sake of dating and it looked like this: start dating when you think you're old enough, experience breakups, repeat the cycle. That did not work for me and it caused immense heartache. God has a better way, it is called courtship. Remember He wants the best for you.

Choose courtship over the institution of dating.

QUESTIONS FOR YOU TO CONSIDER

1. What are some of the main differences between courtship vs. dating?
2. In which of the five steps (attraction, date, courtship, engagement, and marriage) have you engaged?
If none, is this something you see yourself doing in the future? Why?

MY CONFESSION

I am a girl who is worthy of God's best. And because I refuse to settle for anything but God's best for me, I seek wisdom and truth in God's word, the Bible. Not in magazines or the opinion of my friends. I don't have to conform to the ways and the patterns of this world because I am set apart for greatness. I trust that in God's perfect timing I will be ready to engage in courtship with THE one. God's perfect choice for me.

MY PRAYER

Lord, may I be patient and trust that you know, when is the ideal time for me to court someone. May I never settle and date for the sake of dating, due to impatience or pressure from those around me. Help me to be a light and an example for other girls as you use my story to bring Glory to Your Name. I trust that in due season, you will introduce the right guy into my life to enhance my world.

CHAPTER SIX

UNCOVERING WRONG MOTIVES FOR DATING

Being on the go and zooming around the planet has always been in my DNA! I was never that girl who wanted stay put living in the same house, same town or same country my whole life. The first time I ventured out of the nest and traveled without my parents I was only eight years old. Yes, indeed! Here is how "The First Adventure of Beth (my nickname) Took Place:"

Carefully hiding under my mom's bed so that I could easily be seen by her, I began crying louder and louder. Sure enough, my mom came running in. I complained about my head hurting, and asked her if she thought maybe I needed glasses? At that time, we still lived on our Avila farm, deep in the rainforest and hundreds of miles away from any good doctor. Oh, don't feel sorry for me—the poor missionary kid hurting with a migraine without medical attention—because this was all part of my plan. I knew that the best doctors were in the city of Manaus, where my Grandmother Socorro lived.

My goal was to get to the eye doctor to check my vision. But my secret motive was to leave the jungle life behind and move to the city, the place where girls like me were meant to live (at least temporarily). I saw myself as a princess in her concrete tower, trading the unbeaten paths of the jungle for paved roads and all else that the city life had to offer. Ice-cream and popsicles unlimited, I was sure of it! I took after my mother who always loved the fast pace city life over off-the-grid living.

My plan worked without a glitch. I made it to the doctor who found nothing wrong with my 20/20 vision, which I still have. I remember later my mother and grandmother laughing because they figured out what my real hidden motives were: I just wanted to live in the city!! I am not proud of what I did, and yes, I've confessed and asked for forgiveness. But, I share this true story to make a point: Motives are behind EVERY decision.

When toiling with a decision in your life, whatever the topic it's always good to ask yourself, "What are my motives or my reasons for wanting to make this decision?" The more honest you are with yourself the better you'll be able to discern your motives. The Bible also addresses the topic of motives. In James, it states, "You ask and do not receive, because you ask with wrong motives, so that you may spend it on your pleasures" (James 4:3 NASB).

There are only two types of motives: good motives or wrong motives. Being able to figure out which motive is in the driver's seat of your heart is where the challenge lies. On the topic of dating, I want to highlight some motives or why I believe girls jump into the scene of dating as opposed to waiting for courtship. So, the next time you are confronted with your own secret motives, you'll at least recognize the most common wrong motives girls want to date.

PEER PRESSURE

Peer pressure is the strongest of them all. When your friends are all dating, the tendency is to follow suit. Remember, you become like those you hang with because habits and behaviors are caught more than they are taught. Your environment will eventually trump even the morals you have been taught. Pressure from your friends will lure you into trying to blend in and conform. Just like I shared in the first chapters of this book, the only reason I wound up pinned up against that broken down shed in the middle of the Amazon forest was because I gave in to the peer pressure of my friends. Their persuasion lured me to date and to kiss, neither of which was the right motive for dating. Peer pressure was the name of the game I played, and I lost in the first round.

Well, that wasn't so bad you might think. It was just a bad date and a bad kissing experience; what's the big deal? Friends, that's how it all starts. Bad dates and bad kisses lead to roads you never thought you'd travel. What may be cute and innocent can very quickly spiral out of control, and before you realize it, you can't stop yourself from going down a slippery path. It's the small and subtle decisions that create habits. These habits demand consequences and sooner or later you will be doing the things that you promised yourself you would never do. Dating because you're pressured is not a good enough reason to date.

Look around. You are being pressured in every direction: social media, movies, friends, pressure is the name of the game and you must resist. It takes a lot of courage and determination not to bow down to pressure. BUT...the Spirit of the Living God is within you, and you can resist the pressures the world and your environment offers. Be a young woman who dares to forge a path of honor and virtue! Don't surrender to the pressures of the world; instead choose to fight for what is right.

INSECURITY

Another wrong motive girls date is because they are insecure. Who on this planet has never struggled with insecurity? So this motive is one we must ALL be aware of. At some point, we are all uncomfortable in our own skin, and insecurity is just one of those things we must learn to deal with. An insecure girl will do whatever it takes to keep her image and her acceptance ranks on top. Part of this competition is to make sure she has a boyfriend. If she has a boyfriend, a young man who chose her above all others, then most assuredly she is worthy of being chosen. For a while this will quiet the voice of insecurity in her heart and mind and make her feel wanted. Accepted. Attractive.

Insecurity can also cause feelings of jealousy, over-dependency, feeling vulnerable and low self-confidence. These are all emotions rooted in the lie from Satan that you are not enough. If you are feeling this way, I encourage you to go back and read Chapter Two which is all about how much God loves you and how you can trust in Him with all your heart. As you grow in your relationship with Jesus, all of your feelings of insecurity can be completely uprooted.

Your security can only be found in the One who made you. You will never feel fully confident and secure unless you start with giving your heart to God and then giving Him His rightful place as your Lord. But remember it is still a process. Even after you give your life to God, becoming secure doesn't happen overnight. Start with allowing God to secure your heart before anyone else attempts to secure it. Don't set a guy up for failure. A guy cannot secure you and plant you on a firm and solid foundation, only God can do that. Be in-Christ-secure first and others will take pleasure being around you as you become a confident young woman of God.

A NEED TO BE LOVED

The need to be loved by someone is another big reason why girls play the dating game. We long to hear someone say, "I love you for who you are." We watch the romantic movies, see the guy fall for the girl and confess his love. Inside we can literally feel the pangs of yearning as we dream of this same scenario in our lives. Can you relate? Couple this with the experience of not feeling loved and appreciated at home, it only intensifies the malnourished condition of your heart. When you are deprived of love, with a heart running on empty, you WILL GO for the thrill of dating because it keeps your heart chasing love. The main problem is this kind of love isn't what your heart needs. Have you ever eaten fast food only to be hungry an hour later? When the nutrients are cheap, the satisfaction is only short-lived, and soon you will be hungry for more. The same goes for dating.

Dating guys may feel like it's fueling your heart, but in the end it leaves you in a love deficit. You can't rely solely on your parents to give you a perfect and fulfilling love, they have limits, too. As a parent, I can only attempt to love my three children unconditionally. I must keep pointing them to Jesus, the only one who can satisfy what their hearts are truly longing for. Go to God as the source of love because He is the only one who can give you all the love you need. He never runs out! Feed your heart from the heart of God and not boys.

Your heart may also be screaming for words of affirmation, "Can someone please just tell me I am beautiful?!" Words of affirmation are another driving force of why girls love the dating scene. When I heard the words "you are beautiful" for the first time from a boy, who was not one of my brothers, I reveled in it. Let us be honest…there's a huge difference. Growing up, my Dad just didn't often say that I was pretty or beautiful. He's never been great with words. Don't get me wrong: I knew my Dad loved me, and I loved him so much, but he was never an over-affectionate kind of father.

(Side Note: My dad and I have the best relationship now and he doesn't stop telling me how much he loves me every chance he gets. I know he'll be reading this book so I wanted to make sure I clarified this).

You can only imagine what it felt like when I heard it for the first time from a very tall and even cuter guy. Honest zone, here: I felt so incredibly lucky to be standing across from the most popular guy in the entire school as he spoke to me in my native language letting me know I was a Brazilian bombshell. Could it be true? I thought, as I could feel my knees getting wobbly. I had never felt the way he made me feel. Does he really think I'm the prettiest of them all?

It wasn't the last time he would tell me. Like clockwork around 4 pm, I'd skip down to the river and swim with my friends. I would strut down the riverbanks in my one-piece bathing suit culottes shorts covering half my body. You're too young to know what these looked like. Actually, most of America is too young to know what these looked like because we were waaay behind fashion trends in the Amazon. There he stood at the end of the sidewalk gazing at me and whispering for no one but me to hear, "Girl you are beautiful." These were the words I never grew tired of hearing from him. His flattery had awakened the truth about me and how I yearned to hear that I was beautiful.

What do you see when you look at yourself in the mirror? If you cannot see how gorgeous you are, please, look again. Look to the beauty that you are. Don't focus on the things you don't like—we all have those. Look deeply and ask God to show you the true beauty He designed you to be.

What you determine to believe about your appearance will dictate how others perceive you. Choose to speak positive words over yourself. Choose to think you are awesome, even if no one else ever tells you. Don't wait to hear it. Give yourself a pep talk. Get in front of your mirror and speak words of life and truth until your heart and mind believe it.

I make myself stop in front of the mirror, and depending on what is going on in life, I'll give myself a motivational speech out loud. I profess: "You are awesome, you're going to make a difference and continue to do great things for God. You have the mind of Christ, and your body is exactly how God designed it. You are beautiful…inside and out!"

You are perfect in all your imperfections, placed on the beauty pageant runway. If you don't love YOU and know your identity in Christ, how can anyone else? Is it possible there's a wardrobe that far outshines the clothes you put on? What if there is such an outfit that makes you stand out in radiant beauty? Well, there is. There is a reason why God wrote us a little note on this… "Charm is deceitful, and beauty is vain, But a woman who fears the LORD, she shall be praised." (Prov. 31:30, NAS)

Fearing God, loving Him unconditionally above everything, and seeking Him with all your heart, soul and strength will always ensure that you are shockingly beautiful to those who are privileged enough to meet you. Peel back the outer layer and discover you have depth and inner beauty. You will be praised, for He promises it, and who doesn't want to be praised?

To choose beauty over pretty does pay off. Beauty is seen in those who fear God. Pretty is only skin deep. Our pretty bodies and pretty faces will get wrinkled and puffed up as we get older…it's a bummer, but it's a fact! Putting trust in our looks will eventually only bring disappointment. But if we focus on knowing God in an intimate and personal level, and choose to walk with Him, He will clothe us in the beauty that far outshines pretty.

THE THRILL

One last negative motive for dating is to simply experience the thrill of the chase. You NEED to experience the drama that comes with dating. Drama keeps you in the center of attention, even if you are getting negative attention. Negative attention is better than no attention at all, right? The truth is we all need attention because it validates the fact we aren't invisible. If you are that girl or know someone who's always in the middle of drama, it could mean it's a cry for help. She (or you) is simply longing to be noticed. Girls who crave drama are usually the ones who aren't being loved or paid attention to at home. I know you won't admit this, but what is going on in your home life does affect what goes on in your heart…and your motives for dating.

In 2 Corinthians 4:6 NIV it states, "For God, who said, 'Let light shine out of darkness,' made His light shine in our hearts to give us the light of the knowledge of God's glory displayed in the face of Christ." What better light than the light of God shining in your heart? His light will warm your heart, giving you all the love and positive attention you need. No one wants to live like they don't matter. But please know and believe this: You matter to God. Don't let your need for attention be your motive for dating.

There are plenty of wrong motives one chooses to date. I challenge you to always consider your personal motives. Don't be afraid to ask yourself the tough questions: Is insecurity, love deficit, words of affirmation things I am struggling with right now in my own life? What is it I am lacking, that I expect a boyfriend to give me? Is my heart starving for perfect love, a love that only can God give? Am I dating because I'm trying to fit in? Just remember underneath every decision there are motives. Staying honest with yourself is the best thing you can do to keep your heart and soul healthy. Seek always to have a pure motive, one that is pleasing before God in every decision.

Peer-pressure, insecurity, the need to be loved or hear words of affirmation, or simply the thrill of the chase are not reasons to date. I gave in to peer pressure, but what I needed was first to learn the WHY behind what I was doing. Why was I putting myself in a dating scenario? I clearly wasn't thinking past that evening, and he clearly wasn't thinking past my lips.

QUESTIONS FOR YOU TO CONSIDER

———

1. Describe a time you were peer-pressured.
2. What are other motives girls date?
3. How has culture affected dating in our generation?

MY CONFESSION

———

I confess I am secure in Christ Jesus. I am stronger than I think I am. I will not cave to peer pressure or insecurity or anything that is outside of God's will for my life. I walk into the future without letting my past define me. I choose to be single hearted and not awaken love until the time is right for me to get married.

MY PRAYER

———

Lord Jesus, help me to shape my views and beliefs according to your word and not accept the ways of the world in my life. I need your help Holy Spirit to weigh my motives and give me discernment. Help me get rid of all those things in my life that are weighing me down. May the motives of my heart be pure and pleasing unto you, God.

CHAPTER SEVEN

SOUL REASONS WE DATE

There is more to me than meets the eye. I'm more than a pretty Brazilian chick with glossy black hair. Well, after the salon visit, that is! But there is more than the surface me seen by others. And the same goes for you, too. God made us with a body, spirit, and soul. Our bodies are the tangible and visible aspect of who we are, but the spirit and soul are the intangible eternal aspect that sets us apart from all other living beings. Your soul, your inner life is invisible to your friends. However, it is real and of utmost importance in the making of who you are.

Our souls consist of the will, the mind, and all our emotions. The mind is the place you process information. When you first hear a negative comment aimed at you, your mind will decide to throw it out or embrace it. If it decides to absorb that negative idea, your mind will allow it to seep into the innermost part of your belief system. Girls, there is a war going on for your self-esteem, and the battlefield starts in the mind!

Your emotions are the feelings that determine your current mood. The movie, "Inside Out" did an incredible job at showcasing our colorful emotions. This Disney/Pixar movie was the best animation depicting how our emotions operate. There are six basic emotions: anger, fear, surprise, disgust, happiness and sadness. On an average day, you may experience all six, but my hope for you is that happiness is your current state.

Lastly, you have a will. The will is the freedom to choose between right and wrong. Between truth and lies. Between positive motives and negative motives. Some decisions are more important than others, but in all cases, you have the will to choose. It could be something as simple as choosing your favorite place to eat, or on a more serious note, choosing whom you will one day marry. God gave us the will to choose Him or to reject Him. It's so humbling to recognize that He never makes someone serve Him and obey His word. God's kindness compels us to repentance, but He always gives us a choice. You have the will to choose.

Our souls consist of all three: the will, the mind and the command center of our emotions. It's no wonder we are hit hard by the enemy who is trying every tactic within his arsenal to have our souls full of gaping wounds. Wounds left unchecked can be the driving force why girls rush into a dating frenzy. You may know that girl, or you could very well BE that girl who is hurting, and is going down fast and spiraling out of control—emotionally, physically and spiritually.

I understand the hurts many girls face because I am that girl who's had hurt interrupt my life. Hurt will stab the soul and disconnect your perfect world: it's just a matter of when. The deceiving part of soul wounds is that no one sees it at first but, eventually it will surface to the top. Let me explain why being a victim of sexual abuse is a strong runner up to why girls date.

When I was molested as a young girl, it left my soul bleeding emotionally, my mind became a battlefield, and spiritually I was on a quest to find solace—the soul part of me was in turmoil. I write in more depth about this experience in my book, Amazon Girl—Dare to Dream, but in brief, let me share a bit of what happened to me.

The first time I was violated, I was around five years old. Of course, it was by someone I knew and trusted. It happened so unexpectedly, as we were all going down for a nap on a Sunday afternoon. Seconds felt like forever, as time stood still. In my little heart, I was trying to figure out what was happening while someone began touching places God intended never to be touched until many years later, and within the sacred unity of marriage.

Instinctively I knew it wasn't right. But fear overtook my body, leaving me motionless. Years went by, and with each passing day it still felt like it happened only moments ago. And to my horror almost five years later, he struck again. This time, it was even worse. Once again, I was like a prey without escape, still voiceless, and all my strength leaving my body. Once again, I was unable to fight back. Against my choice I became a part of statistics. One in every four girls are molested and I was now one of them.

When I was alone with my soul, I would cry and try to figure out any way to numb the pain and stop the bleeding, but I needed more than a Band-Aid and stitches. Living with the nightmare, one that haunted me every single day of my childhood and my youth, was torture. A prisoner in my secret hurt, I was constantly asking, "Can this gaping hole of pain be healed?'

In the meantime, while trying my best to fix ME, I would fill my life with activities and distractions. They were an attempt to drown out that uninvited guest, the elephant in the room, coexisting with me for days on end. In the gaps between my busyness and sleep, I remember trying to convince myself, "You will just forget about this when you grow up. It's going to be okay, just a faded memory." But I never DID forget: in fact, the incident was just as vivid from the first day as it was on February 26th, 1999. Approximately 5,250 days were how many days I lived with a hurt no one knew beside the one who victimized me.

My twentieth birthday was the day my soul went for a swim in God's healing river. This time it wasn't the Amazon River I needed, or the guy at the river bank whispering to me how beautiful I was. I needed something out of another world—a supernatural encounter with my God for my soul. I was so hurt I longed for more than just a sprinkle of something to make me feel good temporarily. I needed to dive into a river of healing. To walk to the edge and then dive head-first toward a force stronger than my heavy chains. I swam deep past the shallow waters, into the dark blue waters, until I reached a depth of water that was clear as crystals. There were sparkling diamonds all around with God's unlimited source of oxygen. His healing ran through every fiber of my being. This is the same river that is mentioned in the Book of Revelation, "Then He showed me a river of the water of life, clear as crystal, coming from the throne of God and of the Lamb" (Revelation 22:1 NASB).

Moments before my healing, I drove to my best friend's house. At this point I was already living in America. That morning, as I looked at myself in the mirror, all I could see was anguish. I desperately longed to be free of it all. So that day I chose courage over fear. Action over doubt. During the twenty-minute drive to her house, I was not alone. The voice of the enemy speaking lies louder than the broken A/C in my car that was roaring and blowing hot air. The fight for my free-dom was all too real. The battlefield in my mind intensified as I pulled up to her house.

I walked in and immediately started weeping. For the first time ever, I said the words I had only dreamt of verbal-izing to someone other than myself, "I was molested when I was a child." I felt like a heavy load was coming unglued and flying off my shoulders. Then in my pool of tears, a wave of freedom washed over me, and something supernatural hap-pened. My scenery changed as I was suddenly transported to another dimension, like Lucy opening the wardrobe in The Chronicles of Narnia. However, unlike Lucy stepping into an enchanted forest, I was stepping back into the nightmare I had fought so hard to erase.

I found myself in a very familiar place—in the room—where I had been violated the very first time. Only this time in my wondering I sat on the edge of the bed...unafraid! In my imagination I noticed something new, an added piece to the story, like a detective holding on to some new evidence. I had replayed these memories thousands of times, but how did I miss this?

This time going back to my past, I saw that someone else was in the room. He stood to my far right by the door, and I sensed a glimpse of a celestial being. I didn't recall seeing Him in the backdrop of my hurt; there were no other adults other than my abuser when I was molested. But at this moment, I was proven wrong. Immediately I could make sense of this vision and I knew exactly who that person was. Jesus. He was present in the midst of my deepest hurt. He had never left me alone in my darkest moments. Then I heard a comforting voice speak and say, "I was there in that room with you, Elizabeth; I never left you, and I saw you when you were hurting."

Jesus Himself stood in the doorway of my pain. As I came back to the reality of what had just happened to me, an overwhelming freedom and hope covered me healing my soul, body, mind and emotions. Jesus healed me completely in that moment from head to toe! I share my story not because it's something I enjoy writing about, but because I know what it's like to hurt deeply and to be healed. No matter how deep your pain, Jesus is able to heal completely!

Looking back, I can see how easily one can fail and make decisions through the lenses of pain and bitterness. When your soul is hemorrhaging, it will do whatever it takes to get numbed to the pain. For many girls, the wounds from being damaged and having innocence stolen away can be the driving force for dating. In the search for healing the weeping soul, she hopes that a relationship will fix it. Or some girls see themselves as damaged goods after becoming victims of abuse or any form of hurt. IF that is you, then I'm glad you are reading this because you don't have to become your wound. You see wounds want to define you permanently, but Jesus wants to heal you so fully that you can barely see the scars. Could your reason for dating be linked to soul wounds? If so, I beg you to identify the hurt and seek help as I did.

Another wound that can fester within someone's soul is the hurt of being rejected by mom and dad. I met a young teen recently, and I could see past her glasses into her beautiful blue eyes, the windows to her soul. She tried hard to hold back the tears so the other girls wouldn't notice, but the hurt overpowered her as she sobbed. I could relate to this young lady; I knew the torment she was in and how lonely she felt. Crying in my arms as we just hugged it out, she shared her story. Her parents divorced when she was just a small child and the effects of that divorce had taken a toll on this thirteen-year-old. She remembered it as if it was yesterday. Craving the love from her parents, she felt depressed and suicidal. She longed for her daddy to come back home and for things to be just as they were when she was eight. Not being noticed by mom and deeply feeling her dad's absence, she was starving for love and attention. Being rejected by your friends, pales in comparison to being ignored and unwanted by your own parents. That kind of hurt cuts deep. If you find yourself in this situation, first take refuge in your Heavenly Father. Then search out a good church you can get plugged into, and find spiritual parents who can take you under their wings and care about you. Spiritual parents who will love you as you deserve to be loved. You are worth it.

Maybe your reason for dating is not abuse or family wounds, but you have a terrible self-esteem and body image. Your thoughts sound like this, "If I can get that awesome guy to like me, then I MUST be worthy and lovely and valuable." The body image alone does not complete you, but how you feel does affect the health of your soul, so it matters, too. You may have some deep wounds from negative words said concerning your body, words that are making an indentation on your life. They are giving you an undeserved label. Words are weapons and if used the wrong way they lead to deadly results. As you seek to let go and ask God to heal you, I want to assure you that you are more than skin deep.

I have been several dress sizes in my lifetime. I was born a size zero. Telling my friends I was once a zero is always fun, but it didn't last forever. In my teens and twenties, I made my way up the scale gaining sixty extra pounds over what the ideal weight should be. The BMI (body mass index calculator) spares no one as we are all being pushed into tiny boxes to conform. To fit into what society says is acceptable.

I want to be tall and skinny because culture tells me it's the best and prettiest. But here is my issue: I am not tall and I will never be a size zero again unless I starve myself. Some girls will abuse their bodies to achieve what they consider to be the ideal weight. I've learned yo-yo diets can ruin your metabolism so, in the long run, you're better off developing a lifestyle that includes eating healthy, exercising and staying hydrated.

I am Latin which means I have curves and all my fat cells, the ones I was born with, love to camp out and take up residence in all the wrong the places. If there were a remote control to all my fat cells I would rearrange them! I seriously wish I could show you the fat lumps I have on both my thighs right below my hips, settled like hard lard—hereditary. But then again…who told me that my super-full hips aren't amazingly beautiful?! Certainly not God! So why do I spend time believing anything else? See girls I struggle with the same feelings you do.

I say let's embrace the body type we've inherited and accept the fact that we are all fabulous in our way. Let's not over obsess or it will come back and bite with a recipe for insecurity. It will leave you and me in a state of discontentment. I have never in my life met a woman, a descendent of Eve (which is all of us) who is completely 100% happy with her body. Point made. Since we'll never be perfect we might as well embrace our perfect imperfections, right? And please friends…a guy's affirmation regarding your body will never completely satisfy you either.

THE FIRST AID KIT FOR YOUR SOUL

———

Have you ever thought of how much time you spend taking care of stuff? Your phone, your makeup, your clothes, your gadgets? Did you know you can specialize and make money having a career that focuses simply on organizing, cleaning and maintaining other people's valuables? But eventually all your junk gets old and outdated, or you get tired of it and sell it off or give it away. I'm one of those girls that get bored with clothes quite quickly, I inherited this from my Mom. Once I wear an outfit a few times, I just don't have an interest in it anymore. I am notorious for giving away my clothes, but to keep from putting a huge dent on my budget I do hold on to some items. However, eventually all my stuff ends up in one of my friend's closet. Another bonus for being my friend. It is more blessed to give than to receive, right? I give my clothes away and I receive brand-new outfits from my husband so it's a win/win for everyone!

Unlike our stuff, our souls are what need the most constant care. There is one book in the Bible that everyone should read, the Psalms. This book of the Bible gets down and real when it comes to the complexities of the soul. It shows a depth of emotion like no other book, and it validates some of our deepest needs. In the quiet times, while trying to silencing the fast pace of life, the condition of your soul seems to show up as an invisible ghost only you can see. Between school and running to the next activity, you may feel empty, lonely, overwhelmed or even reminded of that one deadly hurt you have. For some of you, there may be many of those "one things" that you've never dealt with. These wounds demand you give them thought EVERY SINGLE DAY, weighing you down at each passing moment.

Suppressing hurt won't make it go away. Relying on a boy "toad" to repair the wounds in your soul won't fix it. Coming from a place of hurt and swimming to the other side of healing, I can testify that only Christ can heal.

Wounds heal, but scars remain for a lifetime. God healed the wounds of my soul as I have the scars to show for. No one goes through life without experiencing some type of hurt. Some wounds are so deep it will take the touch from your Heavenly Father to heal and restore you back to a healthy soul. I don't understand why God allows these hurts to happen. I wish I could give you a straight forward answer on it, but I don't have one. However, I DO know there is healing for any hurt. Yes, there is healing for all hurts, so I implore you to allow God to heal your wounds as He did mine.

Whatever your wounds: sexual abuse, parental wounds, self-esteem, and body-image, bring them ALL to God. If it's hurtful words from those who are to love you perfectly, let it go and choose to forgive them. Go for a swim in God's healing river. Go deep, and as you reach the bottom, bow your knees before the Creator, and leave it all there.

A key to your healing is forgiveness. Forgiveness came before my healing. The first step I took was to forgive and let go of the one who caused me so much pain. Forgiveness is the key to unlocking your soul. Forgiveness is the launching pad that will propel you to believe again, and hope for a brighter future and a better life. It's a choice only you can make. I decided to forgive; will you do the same? Forgive all those who have sinned against you and swim back up healed and whole dear girl. Girl, your future is bright!

Another major key is to talk about your pain to another person. I realize that sometimes it's easier to simply tell a pal, but oftentimes you need to talk to someone who is more mature than you are. Someone who has walked strong in their relationship with God for more years than you. Someone who has broad enough shoulders to help carry your burden. A person who has God-breathed wisdom to speak into your heart, and who is led by the Holy Spirit to help mentor and guide you. This could be a pastor, a teacher, a counselor, or even a relative. But choose this person wisely, and then ask God for the courage to be completely transparent. I promise you, this step is crucial, and so very, very healing.

Your Father in heaven is longing for you to be whole, in your spirit AND in your soul. Trust Him and His faithfulness to bring healing to the deepest places of your soul that harbor wounds and pains from your past. You will never regret it.

QUESTIONS FOR YOU TO CONSIDER

———

1. What wound has interrupted your life?
2. Have you shared it with anyone?
3. How should you seek help to get completely healed from past hurts?
4. Is there anyone you should forgive and let them free from your mind?

MY PRAYER

———

Heavenly Father, help me to forgive those who have sinned against me. In this world, you didn't promise a perfect life without hardships, but you do promise healing for any hurt I'll ever go through. Help me to keep myself in check and recognize when I am hurt I need to go for a swim. I need to dive deep into your presence and leave those bad experiences at the feet of Jesus.

Use my story, what I have gone through to help others in need of healing and encouragement. Allow me the opportunity to use my story to bring healing for someone else as I continue to walk this journey with you by my side.

CHAPTER EIGHT

MY RESPONSE,
THIS IS MY SOLEMN VOW

As I indulge in the movie "Pride and Prejudice," I lean in a bit closer toward my 34-inch TV screen, savoring the best moment. I watch intently, as Mr. Darcy and Ms. Elizabeth say their "I do's." As their guest of honor, I'm taken to a place where all the stress and all the challenges of life diminish down to dirt beneath my feet. This perfect fairytale love story unfolds before my weary eyes as my heart is hopeful to dream again and believe in such things. Fairytales really can come true. This is why I love watching movies.

Not too often do you watch a chick flick that shows the couple exchanging marriage vows. Movies tend to skip the wedding ceremony altogether. The plot is all too common. Couples meet, go on one or two dates, and the next scene they are romantically rushing to first base (or straight to home plate!) Kissing and expressing their passions as the rite of passage into their happily ever after—officially becoming a couple. You don't have to do it this way and rush your love story. Why not take the time to develop your scene and let God direct your every step? **God never intended for you and your guy to become a couple...He designed you and your guy to become ONE.**

Take a moment to watch Ms. Elizabeth's wedding ceremony. Please be warned it's the older episode, so bear with me. Go on Youtube and search, "Pride and Prejudice: Double Wedding." Pay attention to what the priest is saying, because there are some profound truths to what is being said. Vows are a testimony to our promise to each other, in the sight of God and before a crowd of witnesses, saying, "I give you my heart, body and soul." 4 But before you make a commitment to any young man, you owe yourself a pledge to the one man that has given His very life to save you, Jesus.

I can say this boldly because I speak from experience. Making a promise to myself years ago saved my life from so much heartache and pain. These radical defining moments don't occur too often, but when the opportunity presents itself, you are compelled to commit. Making a pledge to Jesus was a defining moment, and yes, it took courage to make such a pledge, against the norm of what a typical teenager would do.

Soon after breaking up with my first bad date, my family moved far away to another state. After days of traveling by boat from one smaller town to the next to fuel up and grab some groceries and load up more passengers, we finally reached our destination. As a missionary family, and since my father was a church-planter at heart, we moved around every few years to start a new work.

Arriving at our destination as a fifteen-year-old going on sixteen, I was all in and committed to making new friends in our new town, Santarém Pará. Santarém was an Amazonian tropical oasis— a little bit of everything I loved: city and rivers. The street I lived on backed up to the river bank. And having that dock was like having access to a harbor sailing right on to paradise, Alter do Chão, best known for its clear waters and white sand. This paradise was situated at the mouth of the Tapajós River. As the waters recede from the Amazon River from July through January, a beach of pure white sand is revealed at the entrance of the lake known as the "Praia do Amor." This place is a perfect tourist destination.

Exploring this city and its surrounding regions was an exciting new endeavor, but I also found myself in church quite often. Going to church wasn't something I did out of obligation. It was a lifestyle, something I enjoyed going to and being a part of. My home away from home. My parents never had to force me to go to church, In fact, most of the time I would hop on my bike and pedal to choir practice, prayer meetings before church, or whatever was on the schedule that week. If the church doors were open, I was there!

During our stay in Santarém, I was homeschooled. Up until this point, I had already experienced going to private,

public, and even boarding schools, all in different cities...
and in two separate countries. I was relieved to be studying
from home for once. Because I was homeschooled, I had
a more flexible schedule which allowed me to travel some.
During one of those mission trips, I experienced a life-alter-
ing moment. It was the day I made my promise to self and
God, which solidified my commitment to respect myself as a
young woman.

It all began on an early morning as I entered a small
wooden boat, whose reflection was perfect in the clear glass
river. This river was so transparent that I could see the dim-
ples on my face when considering it. The journey was about
a week's travel, and the boat was accommodated with hammocks, in which you would sleep each night. The rocking of
the vessel and hammocks were so in line that it felt like God
Himself was holding me in His lap and singing lullabies to me.
When I finally arrived at the destination, my senses were illu-
minated. As I set foot into the huts I would be staying in, not
even the wind emphasized the impact this would have on the
rest of my life. For those days, I stayed in simple wooden huts
with very little luxuries. Imagine if you took away cell phones,
traffic, social media, music, and all other outside noises.

I know God divinely set me up to go on this trip because
the topic being discussed was relationships, dating, and purity.
I was very interested and listened intently as our teacher gracefully unpacked many truths from God's Word. Everything she
communicated made so much sense. I wasn't being forced
into something, but rather drawn toward a higher purpose.

Mrs. Preacher also knew from experience, as she was quite a bit older than me. I just remember thinking I might as well listen to see what she had to say. Oh, and, it wasn't as if I could just walk out and go home— I was stuck!

The biggest takeaway for me was when she challenged us to make our personal pledge before God to commit to a life of purity. To intentionally guard our hearts, body, and soul, as our right to respect the sacredness of who we are as women. Never compromising or settling.

I can still remember that beautiful sunset evening, the moment that changed my life. I get chills to this day every time I witness a sunset. That day has stood out as one of the most amazing days of my life. At the glimmer of sunset, I made my way to the edge of the lake. I had my Bible in my hand. As I got closer to the river bank, I grew more nervous because I knew that I was going to have an encounter with the Creator of the Universe. Looking down on the grass mixed with wild thistles and shrubs, I found myself sitting in a meditation position. Ahead of me was a glassy lake with no signs of disturbance except the movements of small mosquitoes skiing through the still water, and making indented lines across the water.

The air was as though it had never been polluted. Taking a deep breath was nothing but invigorating. The smell of the wild flowers and fruit trees was the mixture of a perfect scent, and the noise of the creatures were very familiar to me. The sound of monkeys calling out to each other, scary at times, but something I had gotten used to. The birds nestling on trees, hundreds of them finding a place to rest for the evening, with their singing so loudly all seemed to harmonize together into one melody. This was the perfect timing and setting to make such a solemn commitment with the One who created all things. In the presence of a higher being, I was stepping into a life bigger than mine, a commitment deeper than I could on my natural strength.

After a few minutes of silence, I decided to accept my higher calling. I whispered to Him, a vow! As I looked around hoping no one was listening, I bowed before my Savior and committed that I would not so much as kiss until my wedding day. And there I experienced my first real encounter with God regarding my journey to be a single girl "on purpose." I felt as if this place was created for my one life-changing moment. It seems like God created this Amazonian garden just to meet with me. I have never again stepped foot in that little village incubated deep into the vast Amazon jungles of Brazil, but what a place to make such a radical vow.

After my vow, the struggle was very real. It seemed as if I used to be "Sleeping Beauty" and the enemy awoke me from a state of innocence and tried to lure me into a life of promiscuity. From the hands of an abuser (being sexually molested) to the lips of a Toad, I was awakened to a new realm of sexual exploration. The choice was laid before me to begin to explore. If, however, had I not had my encounter with God on the banks of this Amazon River, my fate would surely have led me on a very different path in the dating and sexual arena. I had every excuse to give in and blame it all on my past, but

I chose to put back to sleep this sleeping beauty until the time was right.

As I lived out my vow of purity, I'm not going to lie to you: I did get criticized, judged and misunderstood by my peers. They could not understand why I had decided to be pure on purpose. To intentionally put to sleep all my physical desires until my Prince Charming, the one God had for me, awoke this sleeping beauty with true love's kiss on my wedding day. But I was not trying to impress them or please them. My eyes and heart were set on pleasing God and living a life that would bring honor to Him.

The Song of Solomon 8:4 NASB reads " "I want you to swear, O daughters of Jerusalem, Do not arouse or awaken my love Until she pleases."

As a sleeping beauty, we need not awaken love until the time has arrived, the perfect moment. Not to awaken love is to see the marriage covenant as something sacred and ordained by the Almighty. Not to awaken love is to present "your virginity" to your husband as a gift of yourself to him and committing your all on your special wedding night.

I do admit making a vow to remain pure was the hardest decision I've ever committed to as a young teen; it's definitely not for the faint of heart. But it is possible. I have met other girls who have made the same commitment. In fact, I asked two of my close girlfriends to share their stories in their pursuit of purity. They also didn't kiss until their wedding day. So for all you who really want this for yourself, but are feeling apprehensive…Keeping this vow is not impossible! Difficult?

Yes. But not impossible. Check out their stories at the end of the book.

I know what I'm asking you to do is hard, but I do believe you are the chosen one who will join this purity movement. **And it doesn't matter where you have come from; your history can become HIS-story.** God wants to take your story and write an incredible script that will have a happy ending in Him. It's never too late to recommit.

Many women in the Bible have gone before us and taken their position. Esther, for one, didn't compromise. It says in the Bible that she was beautiful of form and face (Esther 2:7 NASB). She dared to serve a Holy God in a pagan world. Now here is a teen girl who has everything in the palm of her hands. She wins a beauty pageant and becomes queen of the nation of Susa. That's a pretty big deal.

Esther is in the middle of all the paparazzi and every tabloid, a chance to be popular in a secular society, yet she chooses to serve God and put Him first in her life. Esther, when faced with trial and hardship, called for three days of fasting and praying. She was determined to hear from God. When was the last time you went without eating for seventy-two hours? And I'm not talking about dieting here, I mean no food is touching your beautiful lips?

She has my respect for fasting and praying for three days. Esther was on a mission, and there was a purpose in her every step. She had a profound connection with God. Her enemies wanted to annihilate her and her people, the Jews.

Thankfully Esther accepted her role and played her part in saving an entire nation.

To live committed to a decision in a no compromise zone can only happen if we get our heart and soul connected with God. The choice to remain pure was and is an intentional daily decision. I knew the decision was a tough one, but I knew what God had for me in the future would be awesome.

Ecclesiastes 3 says to everything there is a season, and a time to every purpose under the heavens—Girls, that includes love. God's timing is perfect, and if you haven't found true love, if you haven't kissed your prince, if you haven't experienced the tangible love of God through a godly man created just for you—be patient. Your season of love is coming. Commit to the Lord now, so when your time comes you—your heart, body, soul and mind are completely prepared. Stay firm in Christ and ready to love someone else like Jesus loves you.

This vow can be possible regardless of where you've been or where you are at this point in your walk with Jesus. If you have awakened love before the time is right, either by your choice or forced upon you, it's not too late to ask God for forgiveness, and accept His healing. It's not too late to make the commitment to dedicate the rest of your single days to walking in the pursuit of purity. Remember, Jesus died on the cross to pay for your mistakes, and His mercy and grace washes you clean. No matter what your past…you CAN be pure and holy!

God is calling you to that secret place where you make your solemn vow to Him before you pledge to any man on your wedding day. Make a conscious commitment to join me and many others on this journey of purity. Promise to guard your heart and body allowing no one to disrespect you no matter how cute or attractive he may seem; with the help of God you can do it. Even if you don't believe or understand what God's Word says in entirety, you must believe this: you have worth, it's in your DNA, noble blood runs through your veins!

Join the purity movement. In fact, the next section will give many tips about HOW to stay pure in a very impure world.

QUESTIONS FOR YOU TO CONSIDER

———

1. Have you ever made a promise to someone?
2. What promises have you made to God?
   He's never broken a promise.
3. Has someone broken a promise they made to you?
   If so, how did it make you feel?
4. Considering the story of Esther as she dared to serve a Holy God in a pagan world, how will you take your stand and not compromise to remain pure in an impure world?

MY CONFESSION

———

Take a moment to write out your response to God's love for you. He is standing as a groom before you pledging His life in exchange for your sins; all your failures, inadequacies, past, present and future mistakes, He bore it all the cross. The greatest gesture of love in the history of all mankind. He's said His vows to you through the Holy Word and acted upon what He promised by dying for you on that cross.

Now as you stand before the groom, Jesus, what will you vow to Him?

"Dear Jesus,

As I stand before you and accept my higher calling. I commit that I will remain pure all the days of my life. As a symbol of my commitment to you I pledge not to kiss until my wedding day. I ask you to sing over me your lullabies putting back to sleep my love until the time is right".

MY PRAYER

———

Now, by your grace, I have committed to purity. Give me faith and strength to keep my promise to you. May the Holy Spirit help me daily for I know it will not be easy. I stand tall with girls like, Esther and many others, and take my place as your Queen before I give my heart to any other man. I pray this in Jesus name.

SECTION 2

CHAPTER NINE

WHERE YOUR HEART GOES YOUR BODY FOLLOWS

Young man why do you stare at this young woman of Shulam, as she
moves so gracefully between two lines of dancers?
Song of Solomon 6:13 NLT

My mom is Brazilian, and true to her heritage, she is an incredible dancer. Music of any kind can be playing and by sheer instinct, she can move her body to the rhythm and be perfectly in sync with the style and beat. It's a Brazilian thing.

Remember when I told you I inherited my white hair gene from my mom? I cannot tell you how many times I have wished I could trade that white hair gene for the incredible dancing ability gene…because I cannot dance! Any Brazilian reading this right now just dropped their jaw in shock. Because dancing is like breathing to them. Their babies are born dancing, and then there is me, the Amazon girl who can't dance. Growing up the best I had in this arena was an imagination. In my mind, I would go to a dreamy place where I could see myself dressed like Cinderella heading to the ball, arriving a little late to make that grand entrance, and meeting the Prince for the first time. Then I would astonish the crowds as I delighted everyone with my elegance and grace on the dance floor. The Amazon girl who COULD dance! And then my bubble would burst as I tripped over my two left feet and my bum hit the ground.

I eventually outgrew the belief my fantasy would come true. Instead I convinced myself that if I signed up for ballroom dancing lessons, my dream of becoming a Brazilian dancer would come true. If my folks could dance then surely I could at least *learn*.

But these hopes were shattered on my first day of class. My body was in total disarray, disjointed like a robot on steroids, always a step or two out of sync and bruising my partner's toes. My heart desperately wanted to be an elegant dancer, but sadly my body did not cooperate.

Each night before class started, my dance instructor would scan the room as we'd line up against the wall. He would first choose a dance partner for the night, and then everyone else would follow suit looking for their friends to dance with. I wouldn't dare make eye contact with the Master

Dancer, secretly hoping he would skip me and move on to the next girl as his dance partner. To my relief, he always did. He probably valued his toes too much.

Then one night, he noticed me. He chose me. Amazon girl who couldn't dance. Why me?! There was no lack of girls who could dance beautifully. Maybe because I had bruised too many toes.

But that night was a defining moment for me. I was born with no rhythm at all, which is an embarrassment to my tradition. I can't make my body move without looking awkward. And now this Master stood before me with his confident hand outstretched before me, "Shall we dance, Madam?"

I cannot articulate how I felt receiving the invitation. Intimidation. Hesitation. An obligation to explain myself. I pressed up against the wall wishing I had the power to melt into the bricks behind me. But as a Gentlemen, the Master stood his ground unwavering in his decision. I was not a mistake or a second choice to him. And he wasn't taking "No" for an answer. With his right hand extended he patiently waited for me to nod and step out to the dance floor with him. Seconds felt like an eternity. All my fears of lack and inability to dance were about to be showcased before all my peers.

Looking steadily into my eyes, as the world was spinning around and around, he said, "Elizabeth, don't look down. Just focus on me and let me lead you in this dance. Trust me." The music began and we started moving. The dream in my head of dancing like Cinderella was unfolding before my eyes! My tip toes were barely touching the floor as he wrapped his arms around me, in full confidence that I could do this.

I was dancing! I'm pretty sure I barely breathed the entire time. I was so scared that if I did anything besides look into the Master's eyes and follow his lead, I would miss a step and we'd both go tumbling down. As the dance continued I relaxed into the rhythm, and I don't think I stepped on his toes one time. Too bad no one was there to record it…My Brazilian family would have been so proud!

GOD WANTS TO DANCE WITH YOU

This story came to mind as I prayed about how to explain why so many of you reading this book might feel a little awkward with different aspects of this purity and courtship message. Our spirits are willing and our hearts truly desire to be virtuous, but sometimes our bodies want to tell a different story. Just like me, my body couldn't dance even though my heart was willing. It was a fight between my heart and body until I submitted myself to a Master of Dance who knew exactly how to teach me to move.

In life, our heart is in a battle of decisions with the body. The heart desires to please God, and to do what is right every day. But our bodies give in to the temptations in front of us, wanting to do the opposite, the out-of-sync behaviors that are against God's Word. As it happened to me with the Master Dancer, an invitation from God comes to all of us to accept His hand and learn to dance His dance.

When God shows up, things change. He finds us in our failed attempt to do what is right in the midst of the struggle of good and evil. The Master of the Ball wants to dance with you. As He stands in front of you, He's extending His right hand like my instructor and asking you the same question, "Shall we dance, Madam?"

God wants to take you by the hand and pull you onto the dance floor. He wants to rid you of all your fears as you let go of control. But before you can dance, you must yield and quit fighting. Give up the urge to lead. His desire is that you submit to His lead, letting go of *your way*. Follow God's lead, as I did that night with my dance instructor. I was Cinderella in the arms of safety. As I experienced the teacher's strong grip, I felt confident while he led me from one step to the next. My steps were being purposed in him.

With God as your lead, your heart is safe. In God's hands, your body will eventually catch up and follow your heart's desire to please. You can't put rules and regulations in place until your heart is being ruled and governed by God. Until your heart is right, you'll see His wishes and desires for you as restrictions or rules and regulations to be broken.

God's Word is asking you to be a partner with Christ. You are meant to dance to the beat of wholeness and integrity, as sure as Cinderella was meant to marry her prince. A bride standing before the groom in all her beauty, pure and holy. Sadly, but true, temptations and all forms of impurity are asking you to dance to the fleshly desires of the body joining the dance floor of Instant Gratification. Temptation wants to woo you away from your true lover's embrace.

Your body is meant to be holy because the spirit of God is living in you. The word "holy," referring to your body, means it is precious and sacred, something you want to protect. Something to be deeply respected. "Do you not know that your bodies are temples of the Holy Spirit, who is in you, whom you have received from God? You are not your own" (I Corinthians 6:19, NIV).

Society is blunt and not at all hesitant to convince you to give away your love, affections, and your heart as quickly and as young as possible. Instant Gratification. And because the majority endorses this way of thinking, dancing with the world is the norm. The message to settle for less than God's intended design is continuously being fed to you. If you don't guard against it, you will accept what the world calls normal as a standard you can live by. You will begin to believe that Satan's value system is good for you, too. This is not close to being God's dream for your life and future. Proverbs 4:23 NIV teaches us, "Above all else, guard your heart, for everything you do flows from it." Girls, get your heart right, and your body and your intent will follow.

Before setting boundaries, guidelines, and rules about what to stay away from, you must commit to choosing on whose dance floor you will dance. A Holy Ground dance floor or an Instant Gratification dance floor? God has a ballroom just for you, and it's magnificent. You're to live set apart, consecrated for a more noble purpose. Cinderella needed only one dance, one moment as she captured the heart of the prince. She didn't need to try other dance floors and many ballrooms before meeting THE one. Likewise, you don't need many dance partners to practice with. You only need the affection and the attention of one. Trust me, your heart and body does not need to dance and play with sin.

After sin was introduced into the world, Satan redefined what is considered "good" and "evil." What God calls good the world calls evil. Satan's value system is based on what is good for *him*, which is the opposite of what God desires. Like Eve in the Garden, as she stood before the Tree of Life and the Tree of the Knowledge of Good and Evil, she had the power to choose whose ballroom floor to dance on. She chose to dance with the sin that was masquerading as something good. What was once a beautiful dance, life in the Garden of Eden, began to come unraveled and contaminated as humankind began to experience the sting of sin and death.

Today we are faced with the same choice as Eve. If we choose Satan's arena, we will dance with sin. Choosing sin as our partner will appear common and acceptable. "If everyone is dancing then so should I, right? If everyone is doing it, then it's okay." If you choose this option, you will be like Eve who lost her innocence as her world was turned upside down.

Luckily, the story for humanity didn't end with Adam and Eve. God knew Adam and Eve were going to fall and also knew you and I would need to be saved as well. Thank goodness, He sent His son, Jesus! He gave us a choice to select *His* dance floor of Holy Ground. As we walk onto God's dance floor and partner with Jesus as Lord, the Master Dancer leads us to a new-found life. A New Beginning. Our hollow hearts that have been longing to dance with the Master, are filled to overflowing as our Creator wraps His strong arms around us. God is still making things new, putting things back to their original state…and this can be YOU. His plans for your life, when it comes to your body and heart, are still the best and most beautiful.

We hear a lot about what is "forbidden" and we tend to focus on that, but what about the wondrous nature of human love in God's intended plan? We must accept the invitation to go back to how things were. On God's dance floor there is a path that leads us. It may be awkward to the rest of the world as you are attempt to dance in the reality of life. Choosing to partner with the Master Dancer, you will grow up into a stunning woman of God.

TAKE HIS HAND

————

Maybe your heart wants to please God, but your body is going the wrong way. Your poor choices are pulling you further from God. But it's not too late; the Master wants to take you by the hand and teach you how to dance and win. Like my Cinderella moment, as I got in sync with the Master and in harmony with the music, the same can happen for you. Purity reflects living for God and being with Him in one accord. Choose to take God's hand and dance with Him instead of the world. Accept His invitation to pursue purity and your body will eventually follow. Is it hard? Yes. Would it be easier to follow temptation to the dance floor of Instant Gratification? Absolutely. But as I said before, you were born to stand out, to be different and in the hands of the Master. So, dance like no one else even if it's only you and God out there on the dance floor.

God has been relentless, longing for you to come away with Him to His ballroom. He's standing in front of you asking, "Shall we dance, Madam?" May your response be a resounding "Yes." He will guide and lead you on the right path, a spacious life in truth and freedom. His way is free from guilt and condemnation. As you follow His lead, you have no need to look down at the mishaps of sin which so easily entangle. Choose instead to look up intently into the gaze of your Heavenly Father, and allow your heart and body to follow.

Are you at a crossroad having to choose between good and evil? On which dance floor are you going to dance? Understand there's a tug of war in your heart, body and soul. But God, the Creator of the Universe wants you more than the enemy himself. May your body follow the lead of the Holy Spirit as you hear Him whisper in your heart, "Come away with me, my daughter, shall we dance?"

You are God's valuable craftsmanship. Everything about you is precious. Your Heavenly Father is a holy God, and as His daughter He wants you to look like Him and imitate Him in every way. You have been grafted into His family. Living holy as a Christian is not God's way of preventing pleasure. Holiness is God's way of helping you become more like Him. Carry your worth in a way that others will want to stare at you on the dance floor, as you dance with grace and dignity

Commit your heart, your body and your life to the One who created you. Choose God as your dance partner. "Those who cleanse themselves from the latter will be instruments for special purposes, made holy, useful to the Master and prepared to do any good work" (2 Timothy 2:21NIV).

God's goal is not just to save you so you can go to Heaven. Salvation is the doorway into the ballroom. As you step onto the dance floor, Jesus commits to becoming your Groom and Savior. He wants to gift you with His dreams and plans, dear daughter.

Step out, take His hands and dance!

QUESTIONS FOR YOU TO CONSIDER

———

1. How well can you dance?
2. How has your heart been wanting to please God lately?
3. Describe a time you struggled wanting to do what was right, but you ended up doing the opposite.

MY CONFESSION

———

I am God's valuable craftsmanship. Everything about me is precious. I have been grafted into God's family. Because I am His daughter, I look like Him and imitate Him in every way. I commit my heart and body as a living sacrifice to the One who created me. I choose God as my dance partner into Salvation's ballroom. May I carry out my worth in a way that others will want to stare at me on the dance floor, as I dance with grace and dignity.

MY PRAYER

———

Father, help me as I am maturing daily, being conformed to the image of Christ. When I look different from the rest of the world, help me to be okay with being set apart as I choose your ballroom and not the world's dance floor. May the desire to please you always win above what my body wants... let me not cave under temptations.

CHAPTER TEN

BOUNDARIES, SAFEGUARDS TO GET THROUGH DATING UNSCATHED

Just because I chose to dance with God and follow His lead on the dance floor, did not mean I was void of natural human desires. Unlike my first day of class as my body danced like a disjointed robot on steroids, I was far from robotic behaviors. I was a girl who had feelings and natural human desires. I was not made of metal and wires; instead, I was born with flesh and blood, heart, soul and spirit. Just because I made a vow to God did not mean all my attraction for the opposite sex was suddenly gone. I still needed a plan. A plan with strong boundaries, which would serve as a guide to keep me safe from temptation's way until the time was right.

The first boundary I established was not to date until I was ready for marriage. I ultimately gave up the mindset of "dating for the sake of dating," altogether. Dating as the world dates is like training for divorce. You pick somebody to date and stay together until something goes wrong, then break up when things go south. This cycle continues throughout your single life, and if you don't guard your heart you can walk into marriage thinking divorce is an option as breaking up was an option. After all, you've practiced this entering and exiting cycle many times.

After committing my heart to God, as I made that vow at fifteen, I settled in my heart that God had me. I didn't concern myself with the fact I never had a date on a holiday or whether I was on the *accepted* or *not accepted* list with the boys. I didn't need someone to keep me company or make me feel loved. I was completely OK with being 100% solo. In Christ my heart was whole. In fact, because of my rare commitment not to date, I had the reputation of being that girl who was hard to get. "Ice queen" was my nickname. And the irony was this only made me more attractive to the guys.

Obviously this was never my intent, but it is proof that young men are truly seeking a woman they can respect. Once my cousin counted over forty-four guys who had a crush on me at some point or another! Yikes! You'd think I would be forgotten and ostracized by them, but there was no lack of guys wanting to date me. I am not bragging, but rather wanting to get this very important point across. When you put a value on yourself and have enough respect for you as a person, it makes you **more** attractive to the good guys…and all you need is one.

At this point in my life, I was living in Baton Rouge, Louisiana. I had moved from one country to another. I share more in detail about my adventurous journey in my first book, *Amazon Girl-Dare to Dream*. Putting dating on the back burner helped me to understand myself and establish some strong personal boundaries, which helped me go through my single years almost unscathed. Now for those of you reading this book, if *kissing dating good-bye* seems unattainable, read on! These next few chapters will give you a plan to help you succeed with flying colors!

What happens if you choose to live by the motto: "Live a little and let your guard down?" This is the message we get in the mainstream. But the truth is, crossing healthy boundaries or not having any boundaries in the first place, can leave a damaging aftermath on our emotions and souls. The world says have fun now and engage in everything while you're young; it makes big promises to you right now, but in the end it hands you disappointing results. A relationship in which you're begging for attention. Feeling like you must be and do sexual things to keep love. Chasing the guy around instead of being pursued like the princess. Desperate to be someone's queen in marriage.

Having personal guardrails sounds so restricted and small, but it leads to an open and spacious life which is the very opposite of what the world says. Boundaries are a safeguard for you. Developing personal boundaries, what I call a temptation plan, will warn your heart and conscience when those lines are crossed. Boundaries will serve as escape routes when temptation knocks at the door of your heart, body and soul. What might seem limiting at first will actually lead to freedom. Keep in mind difficult doesn't mean bad. I'm going to share with you some boundaries so that once you're dating you will have a plan of safety.

Plan for success so you don't fail because you failed to plan...You may be one to say, I don't need a plan; I can stand tall all on my own. But let me say this: even the strongest and the most mature Christian you know is tempted. It doesn't take a deep Google search to see all the Christians who have gone so far to the edge of temptation and sin. NO ONE is above temptation.

Establishing a temptation plan is a must. Remember what 1 Corinthians 10:13 NIV teaches us, "No temptation has overtaken you except what is common to mankind. And God is faithful; He will not let you be tempted beyond what you can bear. But when you are tempted, He will also provide a way out so that you can endure it." There is always a way out, and God does NOT tempt you. James 1:13 NIV says, "When tempted, no one should say, 'God is tempting me.' For God, cannot be tempted by evil, nor does he tempt anyone."

So, don't ask yourself "How far is too far?" Instead draw the lines you will refuse to cross. Know your non-negotiables before you start dating and way before you are physically involved. Evaluate what's important to you. How will being physical with this person get you to where you want to go? Become known for someone who stands for something. Communicate your standards in the relationship, and stick to your convictions. It may seem awkward at first, but you'll thank yourself later.

7 TIPS ON BOUNDARIES
AND SAFEGUARDS

———

1. As I shared earlier in this chapter, the most important boundary I had in the area of dating was a commitment to wait. You will know you're ready to date when you are ready to get married. This is when both parties are mature, selfless, and able to come together and support one another emotionally, spiritually and financially. If the guy you are entertaining courtship with has never had a job or paid a monthly mortgage he's most likely not ready to support you as his bride.

2. Save the kiss for marriage. I chose not to kiss until my wedding day. If, however, you choose to kiss as part of your process in getting to know someone, you have got to know it is a very slippery slope. Kissing feels good. And when you are falling in love, kissing feels really good. Tiny steps turn into bigger steps, kissing leads to touching, and before you know it you're in bed—intimacy outside of marriage. Kissing is not a sin per se, but it can *lead* to sinning. Other cultures kiss

on the face as a form of greeting, but kissing someone on the mouth whom you are attracted to is a different story. I like to call it romantic kissing. As we all know, romantic kissing is the initial phase for sexual intimacy. And starting that engine is like going down the road 80 miles per hour and knowing the brakes in your car just gave out on you. Just try stopping…impossible!

But what in the world will he or your friends think of you if you choose not to kiss? I can only share from personal experience. I didn't date much, but every time I would break the news to my significant other it never failed that he always supported my decision **not to kiss.** The best part about never having kissed these guys is I have no memories of them on a romantic level. Now when I see them it is pure friendship. The mindset needs to be one of treating every guy with respect knowing they're first your brothers in Christ. Secondly, they potentially could be someone else's husband if things don't work out between the two of you. This is exactly what happened to me on more than one occasion. Having purity on the physical level helps to having purity on an emotional and soul level, too. One decision affects all other areas.

3. Hand placement *does* matter when showing affection. I remember telling my boyfriend about where he was not allowed to touch. I was very specific so when a

moment presented itself offering instant gratification I would say, "Hey remember what we talked about?" You can't be afraid of losing the relationship by being too strict. Have enough confidence in yourself, and know your worth far outweighs the temporal temptation that's in front of you.

4. Have accountability! Hold dear to this advice and it will lead you well. Having accountability was my saving grace. My dating life was no private matter. Dating for me was not my claim to independence. I depended more on those who had greater wisdom than me to help show me my blind spots. I always included my mentors and my trustworthy friends in all my dating plans. I'm sure you've heard the saying that, *love is blind,* so true. Falling in love is like walking around with blindfolds; your ability to think goes straight out the window. Welcome accountability.

5. Avoid being in a situation you can't escape. Get out before it's too late. Run! "Flee the evil desires of youth and pursue righteousness, faith, love and peace, along with those who call on the Lord out of a pure heart" (2 Timothy 2:22, NIV). Establish your personal temptation plan. A big deal for me was never to be alone in bedrooms or dark places. I just didn't put myself in a situation that I couldn't escape. But you must talk to your date (boyfriend) up front before you find

yourselves in a situation you'll regret later. Keep your clothes on, lights on, and always stay up right. Basically, avoid dating like you're a married couple. Save all that for the honeymoon.

6. Curfew. Even dating in my twenties, I had a set time on my watch to get home. Be intentional for your safety. Nothing good happens in the wee hours of the night. Have enough respect for yourself, and pace your time together. Move with caution by limiting how much time you spend alone.

7. Set strong technology/media boundaries. Nowadays you can date and hardly ever see the person face-to-face on the other end of the relationship. Words and pictures sent through your technology device is the new way to communicate. It's just as important to set social media boundaries in your virtual world as it is to when you are physically present. Don't settle for the lie that it's no big deal to send your boyfriend an inappropriate picture. The more you give into sin, the more it will demand of you. Don't choose to dance with sin in your social media world. Sin is sin no matter how you slice it.

These are a few points I suggest you add to your list of boundaries as part of your temptation plan. Having a plan in place and choosing to follow through with it will avoid so much heartache in your life. I know you care about your heart and your body, so take a moment to prayerfully consider and write down your own temptation plan.

Once you have your temptation plan down make sure to verbalize it. Hold yourself accountable by telling someone your plans. Seek wise counsel and stay accountable. "Plans fail for lack of counsel, but with many advisers, they succeed" (Proverbs 15:22, NIV).

Imagine yourself at God's riverbank enjoying the richness of a spacious and blessed life. When you live on God's riverbanks you will prosper, yield fruits and never wither. But when you walk away from His riverbank your path will lead to sorrow and pain.

In Psalm 1:1-3 NIV it says, "Blessed is the one who does not walk in step with the wicked or stand in the way that sinners take or sit in the company of mockers, but whose delight is in the law of the Lord, and who meditates on his law, day and night. **That person is like a tree planted by streams of water, which yields its fruit in season and whose leaf does not wither— whatever they do prospers."**

Draw your line in the sand. Stay committed to your temptation plan. I PROMISE you, having a temptation plan will pay off in the end.

QUESTIONS FOR YOU TO CONSIDER

1. What are some temptations youth are facing today?
2. What are some other good boundaries you would add?
3. What are some non-negotiables in your temptation plan, lines you will never cross?

MY CONFESSION

My worth is far more than rubies. I am intentional about my personal boundaries. I will not be ashamed to write it down and verbalize it when needed, because what I do with my body and who I give my heart to matters.

MY PRAYER

Dear Jesus,

Help me not to date just for the sake of dating. Help me to focus on my future and the plans you have for me. When temptation knocks at the door of my heart, give me courage to resist and follow your way out. Help me to accept the boundaries you have set in place as something that is good, and there to protect me, not restrict me.

CHAPTER ELEVEN

HE'S NOT THE ONE IF...

How weird would it be if you went up to a girl and asked to borrow her future husband for a few months? I don't believe the conversation would end well for you. Could you imagine her reaction to your question? What if the guy you are dating is someone else's husband? But most times we do this unintentionally: we go around borrowing each other's dates without considering the fact they could very well belong to someone else. Girls, it's easy to date without counting the cost. Everybody can do it. Honestly, everybody is doing it. And unfortunately, it appears many are going for the world's record—how many boyfriends can one have before walking down the aisle. In hindsight of my own life, the guys I dated and broke up with are currently all married with children. Just because they didn't have a ring on their finger did not change the fact they belonged to someone else in the future. Can I just say right now how thankful I am I never became intimate with any of them???

So the question arises from young people nowadays, "How will I ever know unless I date the guy?" Guess what? You don't know. So the best thing is to proceed with caution and take courtship as though your future depends on it. Don't rush into courtship until you're in a season ready for marriage. But as much as I'd like to believe that all of you reading this book will wait to date, I know it's almost irresistible. Our culture enforces the fact that all singles, as young as twelve and thirteen year olds need to be hitched up as part of growing up. As a result, I've identified some signs you should look for when you find yourself dating someone else's prince. Once you know they're not yours please break it off, because he's someone else's future husband. As soon as I knew in my heart the guy I was interested in marrying was not the one for me, I respectfully ended it as quickly as possible. Have the courage to walk away because your heart is only for THE one as you wait for true love.

He's not the one if he's not born again. I never dated an unbeliever, but I've had friends who have. Tying the knot with an unbeliever can take you through an unsurmountable amount of pain. I want to be very clear here, because most of the time we think if he goes to church then he's a born again Christian. I am hoping that you as my reader, are madly in love with Jesus. I'm assuming your heart has been arrested into the hands of Jesus. And because you are a Christ-follower, you are a disciple and a student of His Word. If so, being a disciple of Christ, you only want to pursue a relationship with the cute guy who is just as passionate about the things of God as you are.

There is no such thing as "I'm going to date him so I can win him over to Jesus, and then we'll get married." Sweet girl, missionary dating or "Flirt to Convert" is a huge risk I don't recommend you take. Do not be misled. "Bad company corrupts good character" (I Corinthians 15:33, NIV).

Proceed with caution; you are not someone else's Savior, as that is the job of the Holy Spirit. If you are already in a relationship with a non-believer scripture says it plain and simple, do not yoke up. So please save yourself a lot of heartache and break up. "Do not be yoked together with unbelievers. For what do righteousness and wickedness have in common? Or what fellowship can light have with darkness?" (2 Corinthians 6:16, NIV).

I hear it all the time, girls saying how their boyfriends are great guys. But the fact of the matter is, if he hasn't accepted Jesus Christ as his Lord then he's not the right person for you. If a guy is not running after Jesus and seeking the Kingdom of God he's not the one for you. The guy must first be in a covenant relationship with Jesus before he can be your groom, a man under Christ authority. If your end goal is not marriage, then there's your answer. You are already 100% whole, being in a covenant with Christ is what makes you complete. Don't give pieces of your heart away to someone else's husband!

I have heard two isolated stories of couples that dated unequally yoked. In one example, the guy had an encounter with Jesus and got saved before his girlfriend did. This was an older couple in pursuit of marriage. He in his excitement shared what he'd experienced, and the girl also gave her heart to Jesus. Now both are on the same page as a brand new creation. In another instance, the girlfriend got saved and serious about her walk with Christ, and the guy was not ready to give his heart to Jesus. Breaking up was inevitable. Now years later she is getting married to someone else, the man of her dreams. I am SO glad she didn't settle. God had better plans for her life. Don't be the light dating someone who is still in darkness, it's a risky move. It is better to be single than entangling yourself with someone who still needs salvation.

He's not the one if he's mostly interested in the physical side of the relationship and does NOT respect your boundaries. This is a "toad" and no amount of kissing is going to turn him into a prince. Unfortunately, when I kissed at fifteen I gave a kiss away; he was more into the physical than into me. There is nothing wrong with taking the time to be friends first. Disarm him at the front end and lower his expectations by letting him know you aren't going physical. This is a SUPER way to weed out if he's not the one for you. If he fights you on the temptation plan then your answer is right there.

He's not the one if he does not respect your boundaries. Remember, it's best if your boundaries are written down and rehearsed before you start dating. Then follow through with an intentional conversation with him, not quickly blurting out your convictions two minutes before the movie is about to start. Make this a big deal! If he likes you he'll respect you and your temptation plan because it's part of who you are. If he respects you he'll abide by the boundaries with you. If he doesn't respect your boundaries then he doesn't see you as God sees you. He needs to recognize he's dating someone's daughter and someone's sister, but most importantly he's dating God's daughter and that demands his respect.

He's not the one if he fears commitment. A sign you are dating the wrong guy is when he doesn't want to commit and marriage is far from his mind and heart. He's not the one for you if all he wants is to date for fun, and for his pleasure. Then his intentions are contrary to dating a prince on purpose with the intent of marriage. If to him you're a casual date, then it should be a red flag for you even if he promises you otherwise. Actions speak louder than words.

It saddens me when I meet girls who are holding on to their boyfriend's empty promises. They'll hang in there just because he's promised them the world by putting the words "I love you…" in front of his sentences. **If he wants to marry you, he'll walk on fire for you. He will be willing to lay down his life for you now, not after five years of dating.** Just because your boyfriend makes promises to you, doesn't mean he can or *will* give you what you long for. How did we get so desperate? Needy for a guy's empty words? When all along God's word is full of promises, rich in love and compassion? Everything a daughter needs to hear has been written in God's Holy Word. Trust me, the Bible has everything your heart needs to thrive.

He's not the one if he's complacent, with little initiative to work on the relationship. If you are more into him than he is into you, he is not the one. If you are taking the lead just so you're not on single status, he's not the one for you. It would be safe to admit a girl can obsess over the fantasy of her love story unfolding and become so caught up in the fairy-tale aspect she doesn't realize she's dating the wrong person. Girls, when the right one is interested he'll work hard to win your affections. But if you must beg him to date you, you'll have to beg him to keep you the rest of your life.

Between the ages of eighteen and twenty-five, before meeting my husband, I dated three guys. Even as an adult ready for marriage, I still made some mistakes. I hurt people in the process, but I learned from it. That is one reason I wrote this book. For the record, I wish I would never have dated them. My impatience came at a cost. However, when I did chose to date I was very selective. The guys were the cream of the crop because I wasn't casually dating, they were all "husband potential." Because I respected who they were as godly men and had no intent on playing with their hearts, the time of courtship was short. The longest one lasted about four months.

As soon as we started dating I would begin to seek God intently to find out if he was my soul mate. I did not want to waste my time or his. That was my BIG mistake. I dated them first before praying and WAITING to hear from God if they were the ones. Don't get ahead of this step. Wait. Pray and hear from God before you go on any first dates. If you dare to ask God, and not give up until He speaks, He will answer. He is present and available to talk to you always. After praying and seeking, I would get the answer without fail. The answer was not what I wanted to hear, but I knew I needed to act in obedience. It's not as if I wasn't attracted to my pick, I liked them y'all!! Unfortunately, I did fall in love every time. In one of these relationships we actually got engaged! My heart broke so hard when I realized how far I had errored.

Then the inevitable would happen: the break-up. I dreaded having to get to this point—my dead end. But I couldn't stay in the relationship when I realized I was dating someone else's prince. In Proverbs 31: 12 NIV it says, "She brings him good, not harm, all the days of her life." What it's saying here is that you are already married in God's eyes even before you meet your future husband. All the days of your life you are someone else's, and he's also someone else's husband all the days of his life. Regard the other person because don't know until you seek God, if he's for you.

If you are reading this and you just realized you are in the arms of someone else's prince it's not too late to act, as painful as it may be. Pay attention to the symptoms. Listen to the Holy Spirit gently prodding you.

These symptoms are eminent in your current relationship if you are dating the wrong guy:

- No peace- waking up in the middle of the night worried and anxious.
- Nervousness- uncomfortable around him, feeling like you shouldn't be dating.
- Breaking up and getting back together- doubt and more doubting.
- Arguing- too many disagreements, no compatibility.

Your loved ones don't like him. Friends and family don't hold back in telling you the truth, even if you aren't asking. I would advise you not to ignore their criticisms. In one relationship, I could never convince my brothers to like him. I was spending more time trying to make peace with them than I was trying to date. There is some truth in every constructive criticism.

Making mistakes is unavoidable. The key is to learn from them and avoid doing them again and again. Breaking up is not easy for anyone if you have a heart that cares. But when you do finally muster up the courage to go through with it, hang tight and put your hope in Christ. Know He will get you through it. This too shall pass.

Girls, it's not enough for your boyfriend to say he's heard from God about dating and marrying you. You must hear from God yourself and "know that you know" he is the one. Even when you think you know he's the one, stay open for a change of heart. That can happen as it did with me. He is not your husband yet and you are not his wife. You are not under any pressure to do what he wants. What matters most is you are obeying God above all else. I lost so much peace as I neglected to look at the warning signs. Only to discover the prince I loved and wanted was not for me. Thankfully they were short seasons, literally weeks. Be prepared to end it as soon as you realize you're dating someone else's prince. Trust that God will bring **the one** for you. In the meantime, there is no need to borrow someone else's future husband.

QUESTIONS FOR YOU TO CONSIDER

1. How do you feel about everyone dating like it's no big deal?
2. What are other warning signs you could be dating the wrong person?
3. Have you broken up with someone or know a friend who has? How was the process for you?

MY CONFESSION

I am Proverbs 31:12. I will bring my husband good, not harm, all the days of my life. My heart belongs to one man besides Jesus all the days of my life including my teen years.

MY PRAYER

Lord Jesus, help me to listen to you when you speak and obey your nudges. If I ever encounter someone who is not for me help me to politely walk away, seeing them as my brothers in Christ. Help me to be single minded, focused on you alone, trusting that you hold my future and it's safe in your hands.

SECTION 3

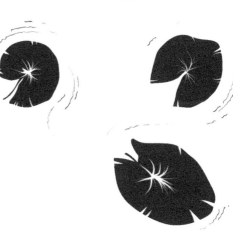

CHAPTER TWELVE

CHANCE UPON

"Imagine a man so focused on God that the only reason he looked up to see you is that he heard God say, 'that's her.'"
Unknown

E very Sunday, I was pressing through the crowd trying to find a perfect seat. Little did I know I had weaved my way past my future husband, the one I had dreamed of meeting for so long. Because of my determination to get butt to chair, I missed my divine meeting with fate. My prince slipped away out of my sight, still a stranger in the crowd.

As destiny beckoned for my encounter with the one, finally our worlds collided. And so, we met on a Wednesday night after our mid-week church service. Most of the crowd had left as I stayed behind with a few of my friends. It was as if God himself purposely slowed me down so as not to miss my moment. My brother came up and punched me to get my attention. Okay, that hurt?! As a sister growing up with all boys, I was about to punch him right back. He dodged the punch and told me there was someone interested in meeting me. Realizing I was being watched, I nodded and forced a smile to disguise my mad face. My arm was still throbbing from the punch.

This time I wasn't hustling to get from point "a" to point "b," and I was present in the moment. "Oh it's a good-looking guy" was the thought that ran through my mind. He reached out and extended his right hand as he introduced himself. I remember liking his assertive hand shake. As I stared into the window of his soul, I felt an electrifying energy running through my body and I loved it.

Height ideal, 6.2. The smile, captivating. Not overtalk-ative, check, but confident enough to carry a conversation. There was no effort on my part as I responded to his specific questions. I was checking him out and liked what I saw. Even though my senses were on high alert as I tried hard to detect anything wrong, I stood there pleasantly shocked with what took place.

I snapped out of my daze and went back to my friends, as I presumed Aley had left the building. Oh, but wait, there's more. As I was walking out of the church building he was heading out himself. This time I noticed him. He looked good in his black leather jacket paired with a dark red sweater. Of course, he walked me to my car. He jokes now, saying I followed him out of church that night. But I say he was stalking me (*wink*) waiting for me by the door.

Time stood still. The moon and stars were all witnesses to our moment— "A Night Under the Stars," and the beginning of countless others. However, our moment under the stars was short-lived as Mother Nature showed up uninvited. The winter rain forced me to take shelter in my vehicle.

I was grinning from ear to ear driving home; my facial muscles didn't even know I could hold a smile for that long. The twenty minute drive felt like I was soaring as I recounted everything that had just happened. Could this be the beginning of my fairytale? It was my turn at last to take the dance floor and dance with my prince charming.

The next morning the sun was brighter and the birds sang louder. Even in the dead of winter, love was beginning to blossom like flowers bursting forth in spring. This was a start of a new season. Love was beginning to blossom. All my troubles and challenges at work seemed to fade away as my mind was consumed by the thought of this new guy. At this point in my life I was working in Donaldsonville, Louisiana and helping run our Dream Center and Church Campus. During the weekdays, we offered a G.E.D. program and other educational classes for single moms and their children.

Four days later, on a Sunday morning he volunteered to help in our community outreach. I couldn't help but like him even more. About a week went by and I got a call from Aley, asking me out on a lunch date. You would think I said yes to the invitation, but I went on a tangent over the phone telling him why I didn't go on dates. Ladies, it had been three years of no dating, and yes, I feared getting hurt again. Remember, I had previously been engaged and I did not want to get it wrong again. I was scared. Fear was all too present in the moment. Later, after that infamous phone call I learned he said to himself, "I'm not calling her again, God. I am just going to trust you." And he sure did keep his promise.

After my fear-driven, embarrassing blurt out on the phone I had to talk to my parents and get their advice. I gave them the description of Mr. Wonderful and what I was beginning to feel for him. I pleaded with my parents to please pray because I didn't want to miss the mark. They knew the seriousness of my quest for guidance. I wanted them to get a glimpse of what God had to say about the potential of this being Mr. Right. I also asked my closest friends to pray, I did not want to go through another breakup.

I am blessed to have God loving parents, so they did what all Christians should do, pray until God speaks. A few days later my parents dialed in on a long-distance call to let me know they would continue to support me in prayer and that I should give this relationship a chance.

I took a leap of faith and laid all my fears aside. I dialed his number and asked if he was still up for a lunch date. I was relieved to hear his voice on the other end say he was still interested.

I had dreamed of falling in love with a prince my whole life. Now at the age of twenty-five, I knew I was ready and confident to step into a courtship with a man. I had spent so much time deepening my relationship with Christ; I knew what to look for in a husband now. I wanted my future husband to resemble the same qualities and traits of Jesus. He needed to look so much like Jesus that I would tangibly see God in him, whom I had walked with intimately my whole life.

First things first. Before investing time in this new relationship such as going on dates, I wanted to honor God at the start, by sharing with Aley the vow I had made as a teenager ten years earlier. I was nervous, but I knew if he was the one for me he would agree and support what I stood for and respect the vow I had made many years ago. I was the kind of girl he never dated, but the kind of woman he wanted to marry. His response only confirmed what I thought to be true— never once did Aley attempt to break my vow. He was a gentleman in every sense of the word. He also respected the boundaries I had set in place to keep us both above reproach. I could trust him with my heart because he was trustworthy of my boundaries. If a guy can't respect your wishes when you're dating, he won't respect you when you marry him. I had gotten almost everything I had wished for in my future spouse. I was that girl who made a list to God recording what I wanted in a husband.

I love lists. I learned it from my grandmother, as you may have read in my first book, *"Amazon Girl Dare to Dream."*

She taught me the value of writing my dreams down and praying over them. You have not because you ask not.

So, my list went something like this:
- Man who loved God more than he loved me
- Tall and handsome
- Integrity and hardworking
- Blue eyes and black hair
- Gentleman
- Someone who would support my dreams and not make me stay home and cook all day barefoot in the kitchen.
- Pastor

I didn't get the blue eyes, but settled for brownish green, it's just color. No, Aley is not a pastor, but I'm okay with that because he leaves the preaching to me. I didn't get everything I asked for, but got more than I dreamed. Only because God is a good Father. He gives nice gifts to His children. In hindsight, two of our kids, Nathanael and Gisele, have gorgeous, captivating blue eyes and black hair. All I can say is, God is good! Our middle son Benjamin also represents us well, large brown eyes and gorgeous tan complexion from my Brazilian side. Yes! May I say it again, God is so good.

What's on your list? You probably don't have one because the thought of meeting "the one" is way down the road. But it is important to dream and write your dreams down. Even if it's a wishful list written in pencil regarding what you want in your future husband, this step matters. What kind of character do you want him to have? What work ethic? What looks? What personality type? Tuck this list away because knowing what you want keeps you focused on what you are looking for in a husband. This will help you weed out the wrong ones.

God doesn't waste anything from our past, even our mistakes. My embarrassing first kiss, heartache and unwanted breakups is now being used to help girls avoid making the same mistake I made. The years of preparation was necessary. I couldn't jump right into courtship, engagement and marriage when I was just starting to become an adult. I needed time as a single person to mature. Time is the best medicine for the soul. To succeed at dating there must be preparation.

By the time Aley came along, I was the healthiest I had ever been in my walk with God. I also grew from my mistakes. I embraced being 100% single. I had let go of hurt and past baggage. I go into details about this in my first book. Healed and on a mission with Jesus was my state of mind when Aley found me. I had my boundaries in place. I knew what I wanted in a husband as I kept my list before God in prayer. I wasn't desperate and I did not need someone to complete me.

While waiting to encounter your Prince first discover who you are. Be intentional about growing up and becoming what God has in mind for you. Fill your schedule with serving the one who knows best: Jesus, your first love. Make a pledge. Define your boundaries. Have strong convictions. Prepare for dating, so you can succeed when the time comes. And when the time comes you may say, "I'm afraid of falling in love." Your prince will smile back at you and say, "I'll catch you my love, you can trust me. I'll never break your heart."

QUESTIONS FOR YOU TO CONSIDER

———

1. What traits do you want in the one you want as a husband?
2. How do you know if he is the one?
3. Where do you wish to meet your prince?

MY CONFESSION

———

I accept the preparation and the growth God has for me. Becoming conformed to the image of Jesus Christ. In the waiting, I'll continue to serve the one who knows best: Jesus, my first love. I have made a pledge. I have defined my boundaries. I have strong convictions. I am preparing for dating, so I can succeed when the time comes.

MY PRAYER

_____

My relationship with God will be the primary focus. As I deepen my relationship with my Lord and Savior Jesus Christ, He will guide me into falling in love with the right person in His perfect timing. Until then I ask the Holy Spirit for wisdom and continued faith to walk out in the purposes and all that God has for me. Not one dream aborted but all fulfilled in the name of Jesus.

CHAPTER THIRTEEN

HIS SIDE OF THE FAIRYTALE

I t's time we take a break from all the estrogen flowing out of these pages and add some male testosterone for just a bit (*Phew*). I wanted a guy's perspective on the realm of dating. Who would be better to hear from than "the one" I pledged my heart to — my prince charming, Albert Aloysius Demarest III. (Sheesh, that's a long name.) He's a bit of an introvert, the quiet one in a crowd. You would never pick him to be the center of attention, but he is friendly to all. Writing is the only way I'm able to get his side of the story as to how we met. Albert, a.k.a. Aley, will be coming into the scene as a thirty-one-year old single bachelor.

Since guys need very specific instructions at times, I asked him to write what it was like for him encountering God for the first time. That experience played a critical part in meeting the one (me). He is going to share his side of the story about how we met. He honestly thinks I chased him down at church after we met (not true, girls!). He will also give some advice to all the daughters out there reading this book. This includes our little Gisele in case she chooses to read this book one day. Enjoy as you get a rare glimpse into the heart of my Prince Charming. Aley, take it from here, and don't be nervous because our readers are very sweet.

Hello There,

I would like to share my salvation testimony which hopefully will shed some light on the preparation that took place before I met Elizabeth. My parents did an amazing job raising my sisters and me, per the Catholic Church and its teachings. I attended Catholic schools all the way to college (attended Georgetown for 3 semesters but finishing at Tulane) and was educated in the Bible. When I was 28 years old, I was struggling to discover my purpose in life but knew that if God was real, then He must have amazing plans for me. I was still single and had a very high standard for what I wanted in a wife. But I also realized that the life I was living was probably not at all attractive to the woman of my dreams.

A female friend of mine I was attracted to invited me to attend her Wednesday night church service, and I accepted – thinking of it more as a date at the time. The moment I walked into the service I knew something was different. The worship music was certainly different to me, but the moment I heard the pastor speak, I knew this was my new home church. I never missed another service and was taking notes, journaling and studying the Bible like never before. I was also baptized there shortly after going up to the altar to accept Jesus Christ as my Lord and Savior.

Two years later, I moved to Baton Rouge and found my new home church. A few months later was when I first saw Elizabeth. I assumed she was already married (to her twin brother whom I always saw her with) because no one that attractive would still be single and waiting. I also knew that at 30 years old, I probably had already missed the opportunity to marry the girl of my dreams. The one who would check off my entire wish list of what I wanted in a wife.

As I continued to serve at church and focus all my energy on getting closer to God, I still longed to be married. It seems like I cried to my mom and dad every Friday night.

Elizabeth interrupting here: Did you know girls that guys cry too? They do!

I signed up for a class at the church that would teach me how to get closer to God and learn more about how to serve the Kingdom with my gifts and abilities. Teaching the course was the girl I noticed a couple months prior. Her twin brother was also teaching the class and introduced his sister by pointing out that she was still single and available. As soon as my future girl got the microphone she proclaimed, "I'm single, but I'm not desperate." This should be every girl's motto. And this gave me a glimmer of hope that she could possibly be the one I was waiting for. But I wanted God to show me very clearly whether she was my wife. I was no longer in the game of rating and dating. I wanted to meet someone with the intent of courtship leading to marriage. I was done playing games.

I needed a plan. I signed up for an outreach, which she was leading with the class and instructors. It was the best community outreach I had ever been on. The exotic Brazilian girl was my focus, my thoughts were being consumed by her beauty and I could hardly concentrate on my task! I was glowing as I went door-to-door inviting people to come to church.

Late that night I wrote in my journal that I met my wife. Like I said I wasn't looking for another girlfriend, I was praying for a wife.

The next day I could hardly wait for the right time to dial her up and hear her beautiful voice on the other end of the line. I got her number because I went on the outreach. My plan was working. I asked her to go to lunch and she swiftly declined and said she could not until she talked to her "spiritual mentors." This was all new to me. What?! I was so confident she would say YES. But this girl was not some ordinary girl, she was different than all the other girls I'd ever pursued....And I liked it.

Doubt began to creep in, though, far from the strong statement I had boldly written in my journal less than twelve hours ago, "I met my wife." Ok, I just assumed maybe she didn't want to go or maybe she wasn't the one. At this point in my life, I was persistently asking God to open the doors and close the ones that were not from Him. I needed to trust God on this one.

Guess who called a few days later, (which felt like an eternity)? Elizabeth Williams. Now all doubt was gone, I knew that she would be my wife. I was all ears and what I heard next blew my mind and impressed me so much. She let me know right away she made a vow to God not to kiss until her wedding day. This vow was a symbol of her purity – which I thought was so awesome. I was so hungry for God and wanted to please Him with every area of my life. I was excited that my wife-to-be had the same type of zeal for pleasing God. We had only known each other for a few days, but I knew without a doubt that a love story was unfolding. It was our "love story."

My days flew by at lightning speed as I rushed home after 5:00pm to change into my best to be with my love. My love and all her chaperones. Elizabeth made sure we were always in good company and never alone in *her home. Oh, trust me, she had some boundaries and I wanted to respect her by not crossing them. I wanted to prove to her that I was trustworthy. I wanted to kiss her on the lips all the time because she was gorgeous! How could I resist? But her heart and body deserved to be respected, and the very least I could do was to wait for the right time. I knew I would marry her and she would be mine forever.*

Finally, six months later, we were married and we kissed on the altar for the first time. We had to kiss twice because the Pastor who was marrying us was not satisfied with one little sweet kiss. The crowds demanded a big sloppy kiss as they stood in disbelief that it was the first time our lips had ever touched. And we still live happily ever after!

My main advice to you to navigate this season of your life as a young single woman is to fall head over heels in love with your Messiah, Jesus. Pour your energy into knowing Him and loving Him and serving people for Him. Try to reach more people for Him with your time, talents and treasure. Write songs to Him and for Him. Think of ways to reach more people that don't yet know Him. Rally your friends at church to come up with new ideas to celebrate the life God has chosen you to live. Ask Him for direction in life. Ask Him for answers in life. Walk with Him each day and you will not miss out on one single ounce of fun and adventure.

And Gisele, our daughter, I know you will be reading this. If the first 8 years of your life is any indication of where you are now, then I assume you are one of the top students in your class. I also assume you are the lead gymnast/cheerleader/ballerina on your team(s), the fastest kid in your grade (and maybe one of the fastest in the state) and finally one of the worship leaders (singer and possibly keys) for our church. I know you and your brothers are still extremely close and supportive of one another, and that you are all serving Jesus with your talents and gifts. I know that you gave your heart to Jesus when you were 6 years old.

My prayer, Gisele, as I write this to you today is that I will give you some idea of how valuable you are to God and how much love He has for you. I pray that I will continue to seek the Lord every day, until you read this, so that I will change to be a better dad leader of our home. I also pray for wisdom and love so that I can share a portion of the love that God truly has for you. As much as I search for the words to say to you, I know that The Living Word of God is the only truth that matters for now and the rest of your life. Since you were born, many people have told you how beautiful you are, how beautiful your eyes are and I tell you to thank God for outer beauty. You are beautiful inside and out. God has given you outer beauty as well as inner beauty. In the book of Daniel in the Bible it states, "Select only strong, healthy, and good-looking young men," he said. "Make sure they are well versed in every branch of learning, are gifted with knowledge and good judgment, and are suited to serve in the royal palace. Train these young men in the language and literature of Babylon." Daniel 1:4 NLT. God makes no mistakes and nothing is accidental. As stated in the scripture above, God used Daniel's health and good looks in the Kingdom of Nebuchednezzar to glorify His name by having Daniel be his top advisor after interpreting the king's dreams. If not for outer beauty Daniel would have never been considered for the king's court.

The story of Esther has a similar beginning. Esther, because of her outer beauty, was in the position to save her entire race from destruction by informing her king of the evil plans of Haman.

The point Aley and I want to make to you, Gisele, and to all the beautiful daughters reading this, is you are worth more than diamonds. You are more valuable than any boy will ever be able to express in words. Your value is not just skin deep for someone to take advantage of. Your worth is a gift from God because He has a purpose for you here on earth. Just like Daniel and Esther in the Bible you are here for a reason greater than you. You're not just like everyone else "normal." You are called and set apart. You have a legacy. Live in your destiny and don't settle for mediocre.

Pursue God and watch what happens.

QUESTIONS FOR YOU TO CONSIDER

———

1. Does your life before Christ affect your future promises after you get saved?
2. Do you recall a time God surprised you with a gift you didn't think you deserved?
3. Why is praying important before getting into a relationship with someone?
4. When was the last time God spoke to you to do something? How would you feel if you were Esther or Daniel?

MY CONFESSION

———

I am worth more than diamonds. I am more valuable than any boy will ever be able to express in words. My value is not just skin deep. I am called and set apart. I am destined and will not settle for mediocre. My worth is a gift from God, and He has me on a mission to do every good work He's already prepared for me in advance.

MY PRAYER

———

Heavenly Father, I pray that I will pursue a life of purpose and zoom in on all that you have for me. I pray away distractions and relationships that want to pull me down and keep me away from you. Help me to not miss my destiny as I seek to know you and grow as a Christian by spending time in your Word. Help me to get to know you better so I can better know who I am in Christ.

CHAPTER FOURTEEN

SNAPSHOTS OF OUR ENGAGEMENT, WEDDING DAY, FIRST KISS

"...for love is stronger than death, passion fiercer than the grave. Its flashes are flashes of fire, a raging flame. Many waters cannot quench love, neither can floods drown it."
Song of Songs, 8:6-7 NLT

Three months before our wedding day...News spread across the deep Amazon basin that I was getting engaged. We flew from America all the way to the Amazon in Brazil. This called for a massive celebration. The long-awaited moment was here. Family and friends started planning for the engagement ceremony. And let me tell you...

NO ONE on earth knows how to celebrate a proposal and engagement better than the Brazilians!

I put on a beautiful white gown carefully picked for this occasion. My hair was straight black, shining as it rested lightly on my shoulders. My makeup was perfect, and I remember wearing sparkly rhinestone earrings as my only accessory. That enchanted night I was accompanied by no one other than my father, his eyes gazed at me with all the pride a parent could possess, as he stared in contentment. I was so honored to be escorted by my dad.

As we arrived at the banquet hall, my father parked a few blocks away to make sure that all the preparations were made ready for that perfect moment. My heart started beating faster as I got closer. I was nervous but infused with passion. I just wanted to make eye contact with my beloved.

As I stood on the steps of my ballroom, I looked across the room; the familiar exotic flowers were perfectly arranged on the tables, displaying their beauty and celebrating this joyous occasion. As I entered all eyes were fixed on me, and no one moved. I began to walk toward the front of the room, following the red runner as my path to him. To my left and to my right, every table had white satin tablecloths accented with my favorite color, dark red. The tablecloths were flowing down without a wrinkle or spot. To my left, there were two young natives playing the violin to the sound of my favorite love songs.

And there he was, Aley dressed in a white linen shirt and kakis to complement the tropical weather. I reached the end of the runner as the song ended, and Prince Albert Aloysius Demarest III came around and knelt on one knee. He pulled out a small wooden box from his back pocket. It was a moment every girl dreams of. I could not take my eyes off the ring; it was my first time seeing it. There it was sparkling brilliantly, custom-made just for me. He whispered for only me to hear "Will you be my wife?" He slipped the ring on my ring finger as I gladly nodded, Yes. (In Brazil it is the custom to wear your engagement ring on your right hand.) The festivities continued until late in the night. Many close friends and family surrounded us with so much joy and love. Most of them were from my mother's side of the family.

WE REQUEST THE HONOR OF YOUR PRESENCE AT THEIR WEDDING...

———

The air was thick with joy and tears as the bride was sharing her stories of the journey. The snapshots of the courtship period whispered in the hallways and the stairwells of the palace. Friends were fascinated by the stories and singles were wishful this would be their story someday. Echoes of giggles and laughter resonated through the corridors, and the workers were busy as bees planning for this unforgettable day in history. As the day approached, the wedding party was anxious with alterations. Carried into the castle were the vases, basins and tapestries that were to drape the tables. As everything was symmetrically stationed and organized, the bride and groom were focused on getting ready for each other. Scurries of children's feet were being heard in the halls. Candles lit, bows were tied, and alterations sewn into a day of glory.

Amidst this frantic primping, the prince and princess were separated in their own chambers and surrounded by groomsmen and bridesmaids. They were dressed for royalty, and everything was set in its place. As the volunteers received instructions from the coordinators, arrangements of the Amazon were created. The flowers sang from centerpieces and fruit was adorned in sweet confections. Inhalations of sweetness were taken in, and the chefs' seasoned meats and poultry were sliced. Butchers sharpened their knives for a banquet fit for the King.

Before the last rose tips were added to the bouquets the day had arrived, and the princess was ready. Set with faith and trust in each other, the future king and queen were about to take their thrones. "All glorious was the princess within her chamber; her gown was interwoven with gold." As the ladies in waiting made last adjustments to their dresses, a messenger rushed in, bearing gifts and a note from the prince. His words comforted her and gave her a sense of peace. As she awaited the perfect moments, the aroma of tranquility and joy rested in the chambers. "In embroidered garments, she was led to the king; her virgins' companions followed her and were brought into the royal courtroom. They were led in with joy and gladness; they entered the palace of the King." As the ladies in waiting were escorted by knights, the princess held back until her father reached out his hand to lead her to the Prince. The King embraced her and whispered, "This day I have created for you," the world and all that was in it paused for a moment of Selah. God exhaled and His breath kissed the face of the princess to seal the moment before the lips of her prince would touch her for the first time.

As the organ resounded, every chord created a harmonious sound. The trumpets joined in symphony as they blared, "What a glorious moment this is, a time of glory and majesty, displaying the grandiose creation of the King." The heavens opened and choirs of angels rushed in to witness the moment. The presence of God shown through the stain glass windows and the light of grace covered the red carpet as the princess's first steps were taken toward her prince. The people turned to look with awe at this beauty, their gasps declaring, "The king is enthralled by your beauty, honor him for He is your Lord." As the drums beat in rhythm, the eyes of the prince and princess locked and fixed upon each other. All the people rose and blurred into the background as the bride was escorted by her King into the arms of her prince.

Vows were exchanged, but nothing could compare to the moment anticipated. As the prince took the hand of his princess, the memory of the lake reflected and the covenant of that moment was to be sealed. Again, the sun set on the day that would always remember, I bowed before my King and Prince and committed that this kiss would be the completion of my vows to Him. This was the enchanted moment that would anoint me with grace as the Amazon Queen. My prince's lips touched mine, and God smiled upon us. "Let him kiss me with the kisses of his mouth—for your love is more delightful than wine" (Song of Solomon 1:2 NIV). I had found favor with God because I had honored Him with my commitment. God spoke blessings into this day because I had remained pure before him. By honoring His covenant, we received His inheritance as King and Queen destined for Greatness.

TO THE TUNE OF "LILIES." OF THE SONS OF KORAH. A MASKIL. A WEDDING SONG.

———

My heart is stirred by a noble theme as I recite my verses for the king;
my tongue is the pen of a skillful writer.
You are the most excellent of men, and your lips have been anointed
with grace since God has blessed you forever.
Gird your sword on your side, you mighty one; clothe yourself with
splendor and majesty.
In your majesty ride forth victoriously in the cause of truth, humility,
and justice; let your right hand achieve awesome deeds.
Let your sharp arrows pierce the hearts of the king's enemies; let the
nations fall beneath your feet. Your throne, O God, will last for ever
and ever; a scepter of justice will be the scepter of your kingdom.
You love righteousness and hate wickedness; therefore God, your God,
has set you above your companions by anointing you with the oil of joy.
All your robes are fragrant with myrrh and aloes and cassia; from
palaces adorned with ivory the music of the strings makes you glad.

Daughters of kings are among your honored women; at your right hand is the royal bride in gold of Ophir.
Listen, daughter, and pay careful attention: Forget your people and your father's house.
Let the king be enthralled by your beauty; honor him, for He is your lord.
The city of Tyre will come with a gift, people of wealth will seek your favor.
All glorious is the princess within her chamber; her gown is interwoven with gold.
In embroidered garments she is led to the king; her virgin companions follow her—those brought to be with her.
Led in with joy and gladness, they enter the palace of the king.
Your sons will take the place of your fathers; you will make them princes throughout the land.
I will perpetuate your memory through all generations; therefore the nations will praise you forever and ever (Psalm 45, NIV).

Thirteen years later and counting, my fairytale story is still being lived. But it's far from perfect, because like all of us, we are no longer in the Garden of Eden. We live in the reality of what happened in Genesis after chapter three "the fall of man." What we do with the tension of where we are and where we want to be makes all the difference.

Struggles are part of the fairytale, and God foreknew this about us. But God is known throughout history for His creative redemptive power. He can turn bad stories to glorious ones. Committing your life to Christ and following His teachings does not exempt us from struggles, resistance, heartbreak and discouragement. We must seek His face daily by spending time in His presence. This means praying, reading and studying His Word by journaling and developing our relationship with Him.

Marrying Aley has made me realize how great and loving God is. God's vision and plans are far greater than I could have ever dreamed. There were prayers and details about my spouse that I know I had prayed for at one time or another and had forgotten. Desires of my heart that I did not ask from God, and yet God provided details that He knew I would need. I am reminded every day to continue to stay focused on the will of God for my life. I now understand that God has so much more than I could ever imagine if we just trust in Him and wait for His time.

QUESTIONS FOR YOU TO CONSIDER

————

1. Do you believe in fairytales?
2. What is your favorite fairytale story? True stories or fiction.
3. What is your vision for you wedding day? Pinterest favorite?

MY CONFESSION

————

My King Jesus is crazy in love with me. I am adored by Him first. I am clothed in a dazzling royal gown woven in gold and precious diamonds are the crown of my head. As I'm led to my King, whom my heart is set on He bestows upon me favor, grace and beauty. I am my beloveds and my beloved is mine.

MY PRAYER

————

Jesus, help me to see you as your bride the one whom you are crazy in love with. I choose you to be my first love to enter in a covenant relationship with. I lack no affection, love and attention from the one who gave up his life sacrificially to save me. I desire to vow my heart to you and all of me. You complete me.

CHAPTER FIFTEEN

REAL-LIFE STORIES

I love meeting girls who are radical, who have the making of a great leader. They are the girls who command respect when they enter the room. There is a passion in them, which compels others to move. And I believe you're one of them! The fact that you are reading this book says a lot about who you are: Becoming that woman who knows her God and walks with Him intimately. Saying yes to your God-given purposes. Unstoppable. And ready to do every good work.

In this chapter I want you to meet a few of my warrior chicks, who are on the battlefield between good and evil, like you and me. Unlike ordinary people, these girls strive to live above mediocre. They have not turned a blind eye to the enemy, but instead have chosen to put on their armor each day, and fight the good fight because their destiny depends on it.

Some days, it looked like they were losing in their struggles, but in the end they conquered wars and stood their ground in victory. And God's banner over them is love.

The first girl I want you to meet is Sarah. She and I go way back. We've known each other for about two decades. She is a bit younger than me. In fact, I used to babysit her and her siblings. Sarah is all grown up, and I can honestly say she is a stunning girl in every sense of the word. Currently, she is married and has two beautiful children. I believe her story will encourage you. Take a glimpse into Sarah's courtship and engagement leading up to her wedding day.

Hello Girls,

My parents had encouraged me at a young age to not only save my virginity for my husband, but my first kiss as well. I considered saving my first kiss special and it became the same level of importance as remaining a virgin until marriage. In my mind, releasing that first kiss was going to unlock everything I had to someone. There were two things that I wanted. First, I wanted God to see that I was past the "just honoring my parents" phase. I wanted God to see that ultimately, the only man I wanted to be wit, was the one He had for me. By eliminating kissing, it showed that I only dealt with someone who was serious about my HEART. Not just their emotions. And secondly, I wanted my future husband to know that I had gone all out to preserve my entire self for him. That he meant that much to me before I had even met him. And lastly, I wanted to make sure I wasn't giving my kisses away to someone who would end up being someone else's husband. I didn't like the thought that some other woman may have been kissing my future husband, but I couldn't control that. I could only control me. And so I did.

A kiss can unlock a lot of things. As a married woman with two babies, take my word for it. Culture deems it as harmless, but a kiss can awaken love before it is time. Just as in the fairytale story of Snow White and how she was awakened by a kiss, your inner want for love and satisfaction can also be awakened by a kiss. I am not saying a kiss is the only thing that will unlock those things, but it was one door that I kept locked to prevent further temptation coming at me.

I asked her to add, "how they met, and how did she know he was the one?" "Oh no girl," we can't leave that part out, it's the best part of the story. So, Sarah added…

We met at Church. His family was just getting plugged in. I was playing keys a few months after he started coming and God told him that I was the one. He got plugged in with sound (not just to be around me, it was one of his gifts), so he ended up being at all our practices and I knew him as "the new sound guy". We started talking after I sent him a text explaining something random. Four months into casually talking and hanging out with family and friends, I still wasn't sure if I was serious about the relationship or if I was just emotionally attached and flattered by his feelings for me. On the other hand, he was head over heels, 100% in love and sure that we would get married). Around that time it was my 19th birthday, and I asked to be sent to West Virginia to help with one of our church launches. My parents didn't hesitate and sent me for three weeks (to get me away from Kevin, I later found out). We both felt that we should take a fast from talking to each other for the trip, so I could pray and dig deep into myself and hear from God. I was so miserable on that trip. I missed him like crazy—even cried. But God still didn't give me a yes or no. Through the whole relationship, my parents never encouraged me in a misleading way. They never promoted our relationship - only that I needed to hear God for myself in this situation. After my trip to West Virginia, I KNEW he was the one. God had not given me a "go" yet, but I knew Kevin was meant for me.

Six months after my trip we felt it was time to take the next step and be known publicly as a couple.. But when Kevin went to ask my dad's permission, a wedding was planned and the date was set. He proposed a week later. After we were engaged was when my parents began to encourage us as a couple. It was important that we didn't lean on our parent's relationship with God when seeking out our relationship with each other. After a week of being engaged, I moved the wedding date from five months away to three months away, because I was that ready to be his.

SARAH'S COURTSHIP AND MARRIAGE

———

My husband and I courted instead of doing the dating thing. He had never previously dated. I'd never had a guy seriously interested in me, much less a boyfriend/beau. We were raised differently, but he respected my parent's and my wishes to stay accountable and not be casual about our relationship. Courting is like dating but with the intention to marry. I didn't want to play around with anyone's heart and I certainly did not want my heart to be injured. We were always with groups or chaperones, never alone together. The feelings that stir up just from two people liking each other causes enough fluttering. Being alone can be dangerous after getting comfortable with your person. There are God-placed desires in you for AFTER marriage, and if you aren't careful, the feelings can be stirred in the wrong timing. You are as strong as your buffer zone. By saving my first kiss, I knew that I was putting up a buffer zone that would help me to resist further temptations that can follow a kiss.

And no, I didn't marry him because he was my first beau. I was not even remotely interested in him for the first 3-4 months of getting to know each other. He had to fight hard while I prayed hard. He likes to embellish our story by saying that I chased after him and was just swept off my feet at his first wink, but no. That is him being his hilarious self. I was flattered, but so torn. I wasn't planning on getting married or even looking for a relationship. I just wanted Jesus. And then Jesus brought Kevin to me.

I have friends who saved their first kiss and those who did not. I do not judge those who do not wait, their conviction is between them and God. Side note: I was not my husband's first kiss. I wasn't devastated about it. I knew way before I met Kevin, that the probability of me meeting someone who also waited to kiss was low. On his end now, he wishes he would've waited, just because he would have liked to be able to tell me the same thing. So, I honestly do not judge anyone on their decisions. I just know that for me, this was one of the best choices I've made. We courted for about six months and were engaged for three. I chose not to wear an engagement ring, but continued to wear my purity ring until my dad gave me away on my wedding day. As he turned to release me to the altar, Dad removed my purity ring and gave it to my soon-to-be husband, signifying the release from my vow to remain pure until this beautiful day.

I've heard a few stories of awkward first kisses, but I wasn't worried about something so seemingly minuscule on the grand scale of things. By the way, it wasn't awkward. As a mom of two young girls, I will strongly encourage them to take the path my husband and I took. I have seen so much hurt, stress and drama, most of which could have been avoided had hearts been guarded. I see saving your kisses (whether you've given it away already or not) as something noble and stoic. Like a queen not stooping to bow before anyone but her king. Everyone admires her for that. Everyone wants what she has. Why? Because she saves her best for the best.

Saving your kiss(es) isn't just something that you should do. It boils down to a heart issue. What is best for me? What is best for my relationship with God? What is best for my future relationships? What is best for the other person in this relationship with me? Is it worth giving it away? Am I lacking in self-control and am too prideful to admit it?

Extra buffer zones and precautions are never regretted when it comes to saving oneself from hurt. Whether it is physical, emotional or mental. Like I tell my younger sisters, waiting pays off so much better than rushing into things. When you wait, and pray and seek Godly counsel, you will never regret it. I had enough baggage for Kevin to work through with me WITHOUT previous relationship issues. I am so very glad I waited for sex AND to give my first kiss. And I know Kevin and God are too.

Sincerely,
Sarah

Wow, wasn't her story incredible?! So much wisdom. So true, what she said, "a kiss can unlock a lot of things." And to reiterate her point, at the end of the day it's about the intent of your heart. Have a pure motive and a commitment not to play with someone else's heart. Which brings me to our next story. She struggled with her future husband's past, but chose to forgive and let go. And our next guest will also help us answer the "why should I," a question we often ask ourselves. Does it matter if I stay pure and choose to wait? Oh, and her name is also Sarah.

I kept my parents very involved in our budding relationship. They knew me better then I knew myself, so I knew I could trust and rely on them as they helped me walk in this new and exciting season. They were there to encourage me, support me, and keep me walking the path I had chosen so long ago. So, with my parent's blessing we started to pursue a relationship. We had spent countless hours talking and getting to know each other so when we officially began our courtship it felt so natural. I had never felt so happy! But we didn't start our relationship just because we liked each other, we both seriously prayed and sought out counsel from our parents and leaders. And we both knew we were pursuing this relationship with marriage in mind. We didn't want to waste time just playing around if we knew we wouldn't work out.

We also created boundaries from the very beginning to help both of us keep our commitment to purity. I was twenty-two and Timmy was twenty-nine when we started our relationship and our courtship was a little different then some. I knew Timmy truly meant it when he promised to stay pure until marriage, and that gave me such a peace and a confidence when I was with him. My parents felt the same way. We went on dates by ourselves, the usual dinners and special events, but we never allowed ourselves to be alone at my house or his. Mainly because we did love each other, and even though it was a God-given love it didn't mean that we wouldn't make a mistake. The enemy knows how to get you in the perfect moment and suddenly you've gone so much farther than you planned.

Timmy and I decided that if we didn't kiss then we could never be lead to do anything more! ;) we chose to save our very first kiss until the day we became husband and wife. One of the main reasons we decided to do this was for Timmy. Before he met God and changed his life, he never had to wait for any physical fulfillment and had several relationships that never worked out. He said from the very beginning that he wanted our story to be different. I didn't understand that, since I had never even kissed a guy! But it comes down to this: Once you've experienced all that comes with a physical relationship that isn't built around God, it's much harder to practice self-control. From the start of our courtship, to the day he proposed, and through our engagement, there was lots of hand holding, long hugs, cuddling on the couch and kisses on the cheek. But we made it through!! Timmy proposed when we had been courting a little over a month and then we set the wedding date for November 17th.

We weren't wasting any time and even those 5.5 months felt like an eternity. The closer we got to the wedding, the more I understood how hard it was to not throw my arms around his neck and kiss him! But we both waited patiently, most of the time, and focused on building the spiritual, mental and emotional parts of our relationship. Saving ourselves until marriage taught us so much about all the other aspects of a good relationship. In a solid God centered relationship, physical touch makes up such a small percentage of the total picture. The reason the *world puts it in the spotlight is because when we give ourselves to someone physically in any way shape or form, it makes us vulnerable. And when it isn't done in a way that's pleasing to God, so much hurt will come from it. And it's not just hurt you'll experience, it will affect others as well.*

The big day was perfect filled with beautiful memories, fall weather, nine bridesmaids, sparklers and our long-awaited kiss!!! It was absolutely life changing! I had found the one whom my soul loved, and was so incredible happy. I felt so blessed. After the honeymoon, it was quite an adjustment going from a full house with my family to living with just my husband. But it was none the less wonderful, and we laughed and worked through it all.

But deep down inside, I still struggled to win the competition with the other women in Timmy's past. It was a competition I created in my own mind, and didn't reflect how Timmy felt at all. The enemy knew this and would try to trip me up constantly. Eventually, I couldn't hold it in anymore and it all spilled out like lava from a volcano. Timmy was completely caught off guard and tried to calm me down as I attempted to explain what I was feeling.

It's taken hours of prayer, asking and allowing God to heal my heart from wounds my husband never intended to inflict on me. The entire reason I'm sharing my story is to give you the answer to the "why should I" often heard regarding the decision to stay pure. The reason to make that promise to God and save yourself for your husband isn't for your personal benefit, as I had believed for so long. First it's to glorify God with your body. He crafted every part of you to be exactly what you needed to fulfill the amazing calling He has for you. Secondly, your purity is called a "gift" for a reason. It's a gift to your future spouse. The gift of a spotless canvas, God paints the picture of your love story on it, and then in turn it becomes a beautiful and priceless piece of art to give your husband. It's a piece that can't be copied, stolen or replaced.

God finally showed me why I had to walk through the pain and the hurt, and that's so I have a testimony to share. It is part of the calling He put on my life at a young age. The passion to share my story so others don't have to experience and walk through the hurt that a life lived outside of purity inflicts on you. It is ugly, hard and has no mercy, even when you feel at your lowest. I now feel a sense of peace and a pride, knowing that Timmy was and is the only man I've allowed to share my gift. And a confidence that under the blood of Jesus all are made new! Don't toss the towel in on your fight for purity. Keep fighting to keep that priceless gift no matter what the cost. God sees and knows your struggles and will reward you for being a daughter of the King.

Sarah's story is a strong testimony of purity, grace, and forgiveness. Sarah, had to reach out for help and allow God to heal her heart from the wounds her husband never intended to inflict on her. Decisions made outside of purity, just may one day come back and inflict hurt on your spouse causing conflict within your marriage. What you do today does matter. You choosing to walk in purity all the days of your life is the best gift you can give to your future spouse, and most importantly, it pleases God.

Next, we are going to hear from girls who have a past—no lack of poor choices in these stories. But one thing these girls have in common despite their weak start, is how they conquered their battles in Christ. In their weaknesses Jesus made himself strong for them.

REDEEMED GIRLS

———

What if you made a commitment to walk in purity but at some point, you found yourself in a moment that is beyond your control, and the unexpected happened. And whatever you intended and envisioned for your life ends in total disappointment, hurt and pain.

Next, I want you to meet Tate as she shares her journey about purity. It is an incredible testimony of how she started with the intention to stay pure, which was interrupted by hurt. But in the end she wins. What the enemy meant to destroy, God was more than able to turn things around for her. Proof that her past did not define her life or stop her from stepping into a bright future. Tate didn't always know Jesus. She was raised in a great family believing there was a God, but it was more of a religious mindset rather than a relationship. She spent most of the impactful years of her life with a void because of that lack of relationship. Like most young girls, she found herself at an age where boys were attractive and she wanted to feel loved. And because of preconceived notions and the ease of taking the path everyone else already seemed to be on, she fell from her innocence. She was fourteen when she fell in love. Only she can tell her story best, so I'm going to leave the rest to her:

Hello Girls,

I wish my story could start with the vow to stay pure like Eliza-beth. But not only are we from opposite ends of the Earth geographically, but at fourteen years old I fell in love and instead of making vows, I was making out. I had just entered my freshman year of high school and a boy two years older than me started showing me attention. He was cute, he played on the football team and he made me feel like I had never felt before. I mean isn't that every girl's dream? The hot, older football star falls for you, you turn into high school sweethearts and live happily ever after? Yup, well, that's where I was at and I did everything in my power to make myself believe that was going to be how my fairytale turned out.

We started as just friends, texting each other once we went our sep-arate ways after school. Then rides home from school turned into holding hands, which turned into stealing kisses here and there. This turned into never being able to be apart, which ultimately turned into us knocking on sex's door. Unfortunately, I didn't know how to put on the breaks. "Everyone else was doing it," I remember thinking, " it can't be that big of a deal." "He loves me and this is what people do when they love each other," was another lie I kept telling myself (although at the time I took it as the truth).

And it happened.

We fell.

It was his first time and mine.

That relationship continued for almost four more years. And be-cause I gave him all of me, I tried everything in my power to convince myself what I was doing was ok, that we'd be together forever. But we weren't, and when he walked out of my life I felt like my whole identity walked out with him. I was a freshman in college at this point, and I just remember the void I had felt for most of my life, felt even bigger. Without even knowing, I truly believe it was God trying to get me to open my eyes to the fact that I was looking for love in all the wrong places. He was calling me to make a vow of my own and although I would love to say that is when I found Christ, that my story was redeemed in that moment, it wasn't. I continued with my life, my story kept unfolding, and my vow-less heart kept yearning.

Tate's life continued to spiral out of control but eventually she surrendered her Life to Jesus. She was in her twenties when she asked Him to be her Lord and Savior. She became a brand-new creation in Christ and her actions and motives began to change. Fast forward to the present, the latest on Tate's whereabouts.

I've been single for almost two and a half years. In the moment, I thought I would never see the other side of the hurt and heartbreak I experienced. But from where I sit today I'm a true example of how God works everything out for our good and His glory. I may be tested daily, Satan is unrelenting, but the past two plus years have just forced me to dive deeper into God's love and what he has for my life.

You see, when you put your blinders on and truly tune in to who God is and how much He loves you, singleness isn't so bad. I didn't and don't need to look for love because I have perfect love dwelling inside me. Although I awoke love before God's time for me, He rejoices over us with singing (Zephaniah 3:17 NIV). It's almost as if He's singing a lullaby to put that love to sleep for such a time. It doesn't matter where you've been. By grace we are born again, new creations; what once was, is no longer. Let God put your love back to sleep until its time. Savor every second of your season of singleness because single now doesn't mean single forever.

I am so grateful for Tate's life and her incredible story of redemption. Update on Tate. A few months ago, Tate met her Prince Charming. They are madly in love. It is adorable to listen to her talk about how much they love each other. She is currently engaged and together they have committed to purity. They have set some good boundaries to help them along the way. They have a temptation plan and both have talked it over together with intentionality.

Next, meet my friend as she candidly shares her struggles when she found herself trapped in the vicious cycle of pornography. I felt the need to share her story as I know so many can struggle with addictions. It's not a matter of if you encounter pornography, it's only a matter of when you encounter it. May her story give you hope if you are in the same situation, or if you have a friend who's struggling with addictions of any sorts. There is always a way out of any addiction.

Hey,

At the age of sixteen I was exposed to pornography. It only took one time, and I was hooked. This led to an eleven-year spiral of guilt and shame and repent and repeat - everything from looking at pornographic images and videos to talking to random men online. Staying physically pure was tough, but staying pure in my thought life was impossible. I would find myself dancing all over the line without crossing it. Still, somehow I knew that despite my mistakes, I was called to be different. I loved God, and I didn't want to hurt Him anymore. I didn't know how to stop, but I knew I had to do something because I could feel the dark hold the porn had on me... It was like an unrelenting taskmaster.

One day after struggling with a conviction for a long time, I broke down and told my roommate about my problem. She had never heard of a woman addicted to pornography and wasn't sure what to say. The few relationships I had were not healthy. I was causing the men I dated to fall by pushing the limits of what I deemed acceptable without "going all the way." What people don't realize about pornography is that it is like a drug to your brain, and just like drugs the more you get the more you want. From that point on, she asked me every day if I had messed up and every day she made me give her my word that I wouldn't look at porn for the next 24 hours.

You see, I couldn't promise more than 24 hours at a time because anything longer than that just didn't seem doable. I couldn't deal with the long term. I had to take it one day at a time.

At one point we even started putting my laptop in her bedroom at night, so I wouldn't have access to it after she went to sleep. It's been four years since I last looked at pornography. I still struggle and sometimes that old feeling catches me off guard, but those images that were burned so deeply into my mind are fuzzy now. And when that temptation comes knocking, now it's easier to slam the door in its face. I'm still tempted in my dating life, so I must set boundaries to make sure I'm not setting myself up for failure. For example, staying in public places during dates and avoiding movies with sexual content. Purity as much as it is about boundaries in life, is even more so about boundaries in our thought life and what we allow into our minds. We can't let our eyes and ears see and *hear bad things and not expect them to infect our entire being. If we binge on music with sexual content and movies, we are much less likely to stay pure. Garbage in- Garbage out. God set me free from the stronghold that porn had over me, but I still must work daily towards purity inside and out. Staying pure is not easy, but the peace that comes with a lifestyle of purity is priceless. I'm so thankful I serve an amazing God who sees my battles and loves me through them.*

I wanted you to hear from other girls beside myself, who have witnessed first-hand what it means to be redeemed, healed and made whole. May their life stories encourage you to keep fighting for God's best for you, it does not matter where your starting point is. It is never too late for your life to become a story of redemption. You can rise because of what Christ has already accomplished on your behalf.

May the Sarahs of this chapter encourage you to raise the bar higher on your pursuit of purity. If you find yourself in a place of addiction, like my sweet friend, know you can be free. There is no stronghold that Jesus cannot help you overcome. Just ask for Him to help because God wants to help you.

And the best news is Jesus died for all your sins. The sins we committed in our past, present, and future. All of it forgiven. His mercy and grace is a gift not something you can earn or much less deserve. You have been chosen to be a recipient of this incredible gift; please accept it from your Heavenly Father. Remember you are becoming that woman who knows your God walks with you intimately. Saying yes to your God-given purposes. Unstoppable. And ready to do any good work.

QUESTIONS FOR YOU TO CONSIDER

———

1. How can you relate to redemption, being given a second chance?
2. What are some other struggles girls face?
3. How does sin affect different areas of our lives?

MY CONFESSION

———

I am redeemed and made brand-new in Christ Jesus. I choose today to set aside the sins that will bring death to my body and soul. By the power of God, I am set free. I commit to a life of purity starting with my heart. I am pure from the inside out.

MY PRAYER

———

Help me, God, to get rid of all the garbage the enemy is wanting to feed me. I need your power to set me free from those sins. I believe in Jesus, who laid down His life on the cross taking on the sins of the world so that I can experience freedom. Whom the son sets free is free indeed. I pray that I am set free in Jesus's mighty name. Amen.

EPILOGUE

I don't consider myself fancy enough
to epilogue. Epilogue is for the pro-
fessionals in my opinion. I'm just an
Amazon girl with a message. But because I had one more thing to say…
and when one has one more thing to
say, one must epilogue.

CHAPTER SIXTEEN

ALL FAIRYTALES
HAVE A VILLAIN

In every "fairytale" there is always a villain. But unlike Cinderella's mean stepmother, or Snow White who was poisoned by the Evil Queen, our villain is far from make believe. And unlike all fairy-tales, our real-life villain is no one other than the Devil himself who diabolically hates the creation of man and woman. He's been on a mission, seeking to destroy our stories with the end goal to forever separate us from the love of God. Jesus was clear in telling us the reality of the fight between good and evil. He never promised a life without an enemy, but He did say, "In this world, you will have trouble. But take heart! I have overcome the world" (John 16:33, NIV).

Committing your life to Christ and following His teachings does not exempt you from the enemy's opposition. You are a threat to the devil. And we need to fight and fight to win. How does someone fight to win? There are three things I want to share with you that I've learned, on how to fight against the villain—the enemy of our soul.

First, don't fight the enemy on his battlefield. We must bring our opponent to a realm he cannot fight well. We disarm him by bringing our battles to higher grounds, God's battlefield. Take an eagle for example. The eagle does not fight her enemy, the snake, on the ground. She brings her predator to the sky; she changes the backdrop of her battlefield. With its' powerful claws, the eagle grabs the snake and releases the catch in mid-air. Snakes can't fly, right? You see, the serpent on the ground is powerful and deadly. The snake can inflict a fatal bite, but in the air it's completely disarmed and unable to strike.

Like an eagle, bring your battle to higher grounds, to the Heavens in prayer. And God in His faithfulness will take on your opponent. God will fight with you. Don't fight your enemy on the ground, change your battlefield. Bring it up higher. When earthly things fail you, in the dust of disappointments, God's Heavenly things will never fail you. You can have victory over death's sting.

Yet those who wait for the Lord
Will gain new strength;
They will mount up with wings like eagles,
They will run and not get tired,
They will walk and not become weary.
(Isaiah 40:31, NASB)

Second, we fight our villain by staying close to the LORD of hosts, the God of the armies of Israel (1 Samuel 17:45 NIV). Spending time with God by praying, reading and studying His Word are all ways to stay close to God. Not only will we learn more about the God of heaven's armies, but He will also teach us how to fight our opponent. God has never lost a battle. He is eager to teach us how to fight and win. And, our weapon of choice needs to be His Word—the Bible. The art of reading (Jesus) is a lost art, but we can't afford to lose this weapon "the power of reading His Word" or we'll suffer a significant loss in our personal lives. Let's refuse to become a generation who knows not God nor of the wondrous things He has done. We can't afford illiteracy when it comes to the Word, which is the SWORD of the Spirit (Ephesians 6:17 NIV).

Not long after we said "I do" inside the castle on the river aka "Louisiana's Old State Capital," which was built in 1929 with construction to look and function like a castle, we faced battles like most couples do. But we knew we were not alone. We chose to grow and learn from God regarding the art of winning the battles that came our way. The same God who was with me when I was single was with us in our marriage. Right by our side in every season. Perhaps one day I'll write another book, about my many battles. I seriously think I'm a warrior princess: like "Wonder Woman" who can ride a horse (preferably white stallions) with the archery skill sets of Katniss Everdeen in "The Hunger Games." I do have an imagination. But, in real-life, I am a warrior, God's Princess Bride, who fights a losing enemy and his army. I have read "The End" in the book of Revelation, I win. And maybe, just maybe, I am writing to a generation of girls who are warriors in their battlefields. Girls who have decided to wake up and not let the enemy hold them hostage any longer.

Thirdly, I must say worship, is a must weapon of choice to win. Before circumstances begin to turn around worship must take place. Instead of complaining and murmuring, build an altar of thanksgiving. An altar is a place where you go before God to present Him with a gift, the gift of worship and thanksgiving. An altar of thanksgiving changes the atmosphere from negativity to praise. God is near when Thanksgiving is going up. He inhabits the praise of His people.

There's a passage in the Bible where Paul and Silas have been beaten and thrown in jail, but instead of crying and feeling sorry for themselves they opened their mouths and began to pray and worship. Look what happened to them, "About midnight Paul and Silas were praying and singing hymns to God, and the other prisoners were listening to them. Suddenly there was such a violent earthquake that the foundations of the prison were shaken. At once, all the prison doors flew open, and everyone's chains came loose" (Acts 16:25-27 NIV). Something happens when we open our mouths to worship our Creator. Chains are ripped off. Doors swing wide open. Our views shift from looking down at the circumstances to looking up, and seeing how big our God is. Lift your head high, and begin to see yourself in a different light. We all go through the storms, but like eagles we are meant to soar above the enemy's camp. Maybe you are going through depression, or even cutting yourself thinking you deserve nothing more than punishment. You may be in an awful hard spot, and your life is not where you thought it should be.

Choose to be a princess who puts on the wardrobe of a WARRIOR. If you've been held hostage in the enemy's camp, it's time to dust yourself off and take flight. Believe that you can fly. Soar baby girl! Take your battle to higher grounds and fight with God on your side. Go live God's dream— alive and full of adventure, risks, and leaps of faith. There's a warrior inside of you!

THANK YOU

I dedicate this section of the book to personally thank ALL my friends and family, everyone who has made this dream a reality. To yawl I send this book with my deepest thanks and like we say it in Português, "Muito Obrigada":

To my hubby, my prince, who's responsible for capturing my dreams years ago, and fanning the flames by refusing to let me give up. For the past six months, as I've spent countless hours on this book with my butt on a chair, Aley has held down the fort. He has folded loads of clothes and picked the kids up from school, so that I could write till 3:20 pm. Fed our children (mostly Canes fried chicken), and did homework with them so I could keep writing. He is the type of husband you want to marry and cherish! Aley has also been my biggest encourager. The numerous times I wanted to give up I'd ask him, "Do you think writing this book is worth it?" And his reply was always, "Of course it's worth it because Jesus is worth it."

To my editor and friend, Molly Venzke. She was an answer to prayers. I was literally on my knees asking God to send me an angel or else I'd throw in the towel—peace out. But God was already lining things up. Within minutes of me sending her an email asking for HELP she replied YES (without looking at the manuscript). However, she had no idea how rough my first draft was. Molly also became my greatest coach in the process. Over the past six months, she's given me phone workshops, taught me to slow down when writing (take your time Elizabeth, read SLOWLY). And after major rounds of editing she has continued as a constant cheerleader in my corner. Thank you, Molly for being a big sister, never giving up on me and making time for me during your own very own successful career. (Go check out Molly's awesome book "Caged No More" which has been turned into a movie, a must see, with the same title).

To my graphic designer, Rob Gros, whose stunning artwork has made this cover so irresistible—eye catching! The ease of you reading each page is due in part to his skills.

To my church family. They have been the crowd in the stands. Their anthem of love has been sung over me since the very beginning of this long process. Holding me accountable to keep going.

To my extended family. I owe my parents and my four brothers a huge thank you. Because of my heritage I have a story. Their obedience to the call of God in their lives has made my adventures in the Amazon rainforest easy to chronicle. To my grandparents' legacy, they sacrificed all in the name of Jesus and His mission.

To you, dear reader, for choosing to come along on this journey. Your commitment to coming this far with me is humbling.

To Jesus who saved me eternally and rescued me from the grips of hurt and pain. I love you so much, even the mention of your name brings me to tears. I can't fathom what it's like to live without you. Thank you for loving me and never breaking my heart. I love you with every fiber of my being, and I cannot wait to see you face to face one day soon.

BIBLIOGRAPHY

Elizabeth S. Demarest, Amazon Girl Dare to Dream
(Bloomington, IN: WestBow Press, 2014).

Scripture taken from the NEW AMERICAN STANDARD
BIBLE, Copyright 1999, 2000, 2002, 2003, 2009
by Holman Bible Publishes. Used by permission.

THE HOLY BIBLE, NEW INTERNATIONAL
VERSION, NIV Copyright 1973, 1978, 1984, 2011 by
Biblica, Inc. Used by permission.
All rights reserved worldwide.

Scripture quotations marked (NLT) are taken from the Holy
Bible, New Living Translation, copyright 1996, 2004, 2007 by
Tyndale House Foundation. Used by permission of
Tyndale House Publishers, Inc., Carol Stream, Illinois 60188.
All rights reserved.

"Song of Solomon for Students: Tommy Nelson:
The HUB." RightNow Media,
www.rightnowmedia.org/Content/Series/135.

WORKS CITED

1. "The Princess Diaries" movie (2001).
2. Beth L. Bailey, From Front Porch to Back Seat: Courtship in Twentieth-century America (Baltimore: Johns Hopkins UP, 1988).
3. Beth L. Bailey, From Front Porch to Back Seat: Courtship in Twentieth-century America (Baltimore: Johns Hopkins UP, 1988).
4. BBCWorldwide. YouTube, YouTube, 11 Feb. 2008, www.youtube.com.

Made in the USA
Middletown, DE
17 August 2024

59250312R00106